W9-BOO-188

CARD GAMES
ENCYCLOPEDIA

CARD GAMES

ENCYCLOPEDIA

OVER 100 DIFFERENT CARD GAMES, INCLUDING
A SPECIALIZED SECTION ON POKER

p

This is a Parragon Publishing Book

This edition published in 2006

Parragon Publishing

Queen Street House

4 Queen Street

Bath BA1 1HE, UK

This edition designed by Design Principals

Text by Sue Barraclough, Louis Canasta and Stewart Reuben

Edited by Sue Barraclough

ISBN: 1-40547-137-9

Printed in China

Contents

JOKER

Introduction

This book contains a fantastic range of card games along with their many variations—from classic games of skill such as Bridge and Poker for the more serious card player, to fun family and party games for all ages. It is an easy reference book for the card game novice to help them to find a game to suit a certain number of players and any occasion, as well as providing more challenging games to interest the more experienced card player. The games are grouped into sections such as Patience games for one player, or games for two, or families of games that are played in a similar way, so it's easy to find old favorites or to try something new.

A SHORT HISTORY OF PLAYING CARDS

Playing cards have been around since at least the 14th century but their exact origins are hazy and highly debatable. They are thought by many to have been made first in China, which seems logical because China was the first country to manufacture paper. Some theories trace their roots back to Tarot cards, while just as many people believe that Tarot cards were developed from an existing set of cards. However, most people agree that playing cards spread from the East via Persia, India and Egypt, with religious and other significant symbols being used, adapted or discarded as the cards were changed to suit particular games and fashions.

It was only when the cards spread to Europe that the courtly figures—the kings and queens and their attendants—that we recognize today developed. At one time the kings were said to represent the great kings: David, Alexander, Charlemagne and Caesar. Playing cards have featured many different suit symbols and in Germany, today, the suits are hearts, bells, leaves and acorns, while in Spain they feature clubs, coins, swords and cups.

It is easy to imagine how soldiers and sailors returned home with actual cards or maybe just memories and sketches of cards they had seen and games they had played on their travels. And how these, often incomplete, details were passed on to friends and family. Thus symbols would have changed as they were passed along and meanings would often have been lost in translation. And so playing cards changed and evolved.

The first playing cards were hand-made and hand-decorated and only the very wealthy could afford to own them. The invention of woodcuts in 14th century Europe made producing them in larger quantities possible, and playing cards found their way into ordinary households. The suits—hearts, diamonds, spades and clubs—are French in origin. The simple symbols and flat colors made them much easier to recognize and reproduce, and made manufacturing them on a larger scale feasible.

The Joker is thought to have been introduced to the deck in the USA in around 1870. Euchre players were tinkering with the rules and decided an extra trump card might come in handy. He was first named "Best Bower" and it was only later that he became known as the Jolly Joker. The joker is generally used now as a wild card to add a little spice to a game.

The fifty-two card deck consisting of kings, queens and jacks and the numbered suits of hearts, clubs, spades and diamonds are now recognized and played with all over the world.

PLAYING-CARD GAMES THROUGH THE AGES

Games of skill and gambling games of chance have come and gone through the centuries. There are many games that were hugely popular for many years—such as Noddy (an ancestor of Cribbage) in Tudor times—which then fell from grace and are all but forgotten now. Some games such as Cribbage and Piquet have been around for hundreds of years, and while variations have been devised, the basic structure of the

games have continued and remained popular. Many card games, such as Whist for example, have changed and developed into new games like Bridge, as well as spawning a myriad of variations.

Many card players will insist a rule is correct "according to Hoyle" as if that proves it is indisputable. However, the idea that Hoyle set the official rules for all games is a bit of a myth. Hoyle wrote a treatise on Whist in 1742 which was very successful, but when Hoyle died in 1769 he had only devised half a dozen games and his specialty was strategy, not rules.

One of the best things about card games is that the rules are pretty much there to be broken, as has been proved through the ages. Card games have changed, evolved and probably improved, over the years, because they have been adapted, and as long as all the players are clear about the rules before you start a game, you can be as creative as you like.

HOW TO USE THIS BOOK

At the beginning of each card game, there is quick-reference list providing a breakdown of all the important information for each game to get you started. It also includes guidance on how suitable the game is for children or for gambling. And gives a quick indication of how difficult the game is to learn—the simplicity factor, and also how much brain power it requires—the skill factor.

Reference list numbering system

1	2	3	4	5	6	7	8	9	10
low				average					high

CHAPTER 1

Bridge and Whist

In their most basic forms Bridge and Whist are pretty simple trumps and tricks games. Fifty-two cards are dealt to the four players, trumps are set, and the winner is the player to win most of the thirteen tricks. Whist variations include scoring quirks or gambling elements to make play more interesting. While Bridge largely differs in its bidding and scoring, and Contract Bridge has the added interest of the players being paired off.

Bridge

PLAYERS: FOUR

DECK: FULL

ACES: HIGH

SCORE SHEET: YES

ORIGIN: GREAT BRITAIN

SIMPLICITY FACTOR: GAME–8. BETTING–8

SKILL FACTOR: GAME–5. BETTING–8

SUITABLE FOR CHILDREN: 2

SUITABLE FOR GAMBLING: 6

A little over a hundred years old, Bridge evolved out of Whist. It is distinguished from that game by the bidding and scoring system, and the fact that it is played by four people who have been paired off. Explained as the main game here is Contract Bridge, by far the most popular version of the game, in which "contracts" are "bid" for by the partnerships, who then attempt to make the number of tricks they have declared they will. Bridge is a game of enormous subtlety and the best partnerships are those who have been playing together for a long time. There has been an entire library of books written on the game and how best to play it, what follows is merely the rules.

BIDDING

All cards are dealt out to the four players and bidding takes place as soon as players have inspected their hands. In spite of them operating in tandem, there is supposed to be no communication between the partners once the game gets underway. Players are bidding for the contract, which is a declaration of how many tricks they believe their partnership can make. As they bid, they denote which suit will be trumps, or can bid "no trumps" which means exactly that. Each contract declaration has its own ranking of value, depending on which suit, if any, is being called as trumps. As the bidding goes round the table, it escalates until all except one has "passed" and the player who makes the most valuable bid becomes the "declarer". Together with his partner, the declarer will then try to make the contract.

Each bid specifies how many tricks over the "book" (six tricks) partnerships believe they can make. In Bridge there is a hierarchy among the suits when they are called as trumps, with a "no trumps" bid outranking them all. The bids in descending order are:

1) Seven no trumps (13 tricks, aka a grand slam, with all suits equal)
2) Seven spades (13 tricks with spades as trumps)
3) Seven hearts (13 tricks with hearts as trumps)
4) Seven diamonds (13 tricks with diamonds as trumps)
5) Seven clubs (13 tricks with clubs as trumps).

This will continue down to the lowest bid which is One clubs—seven tricks with clubs as trumps.

If players don't want to bid in a round of the auction they can say "pass" and still bid in a later round, but if all four players pass on the first round, the cards are collected, shuffled and re-dealt. As well as passing or outbidding rivals, players can "double" or "redouble" opponents' calls. To double a bid means to assert that your partnership could prevent the bid being achieved if it became a contract. If the players achieve this,

A short history of Bridge

For such an internationally popular game, it is curious that nobody really knows where the name came from. It may have developed from a Russian or a Turkish word, but it certainly has nothing to do with a bridge as we know it!

Bridge dates back to the 16th century and it is clear that it developed from the Whist family. The game changed and developed as card games tend to do, and by the time it was introduced to the United States in the 1890s, it had become known as Bridge. The game continued to change until millionaire Harold Vanderbilt settled down to perfect the game, during a long winter cruise in 1925. He wrote down rules and other principles and even devised a scoring table. His adaptations shaped the game of Contract Bridge that we know today and which has become one of the most popular forms of Bridge.

the points scored by them will be doubled. If they fail to stop the contract being made, the declarer's points are doubled. If a potential declarer has had his bid doubled and the bidding comes back round to him without being raised, he can call "redouble". This means that should the bid become a contract, the scores are doubled from the double—quadruple what they would have originally been.

PLAYING

A full deck is dealt out and the declarer leads. As soon as he has played his first card his partner lays his hand face-upward on the table for the declarer to play that hand for him. This hand is called the "dummy". Tricks are played for as in Whist—won by the highest card played in the lead suit, or by trumping if there has been a trump suit designated. Tricks are collected in front of the declarer and one member of the other partnership. Once all 13 have been played the scores for that game are tallied up and entered on to the score sheet.

SCORING

Bridge score sheets are divided vertically and horizontally. The vertical line separates each partnership's scores and are usually headed "We" and "They" as it's advisable for both teams to keep a record of the scores. Each partnership can then score points that are recorded below and above the horizontal line.

Below the line points are for tricks won in completion of the contract once the book has been made, so they are for each trick made over six. Only the declaring partnership can win these trick points, and the values of the tricks depend on the suit called as trumps, and correspond to the hierarchy in the bidding process:

- Clubs and diamonds are worth 20 points per trick, 40 when doubled and 80 when redoubled
- Hearts and spades are worth 30 points per trick, 60 when doubled and 120 when redoubled
- No trumps are worth 40 points per trick, 80 when doubled and 160 when redoubled for the first trick and 30, 60 or 120 for subsequent tricks.

Above the line are "premium points". The values change quite drastically once a partnership becomes "vulnerable". This occurs after a partnership has won one game towards a best-of-three rubber—both partnerships will be vulnerable once they've each won one game. The premium points are as follows:

Grand Slam or Small Slam

Completing a grand slam—1000; if vulnerable—1500.
Completing a small slam (a bid of six, so 12 tricks have to be taken)—500; if vulnerable—750.

Overtricks

For each trick taken over the number required by the contract:

- Overtricks—the value of the trick
- Doubled overtricks—100; if vulnerable—200 (regardless of the trick's value)
- Re-doubled overtricks 200; if vulnerable—400 (regardless of the trick's value).

Undertricks:

These are added to opponent's score:

- First undertrick—50; if vulnerable—100
- Subsequent undertricks—50; if vulnerable -100
- First doubled undertrick—100; if vulnerable—200
- Subsequent doubled undertricks—200; if vulnerable—300
- First redoubled undertrick—200; if vulnerable—400
- Subsequent redoubled undertricks—400; if vulnerable—600.

Win Bonuses

- For making a doubled or redoubled contract—50 (vulnerable or otherwise).
- For winning a three-game rubber 2-0—700.
- For winning a three-game rubber 2-1—500.
- For winning one game in an abandoned rubber—300.
- For having the only score in an abandoned game—50.

Honor Cards

Extra points are awarded before any cards are played for players holding what are known as honor cards in their original hands—this is for individual hands, not partnerships:

• A, K, Q, J, 10 of trumps—150
• Any permutation of four from the above—100
• Four aces (in a no trump game)—150.

A running score of the below-the-line points is kept, they are added up after each hand and the first team to 100 trick points wins the game. When a partnership has won two games the rubber is decided by whichever has the higher total of trick and premium points when their scores from all of the games are added together.

BETTING

A pre-agreed cash value for points is the best way, with amounts paid on the difference between the winning and losing totals.

Variations

AUCTION BRIDGE

An earlier game than Contract Bridge. Although the rules are the same, the scoring schedule is completely different. There is no vulnerability and all tricks made over the book are scored below the line, providing the declarer has made the contract—even if they are over the contract. Trick scores are:

• Each trick won after book has been made—clubs—6; diamonds—7; hearts—8; spades—9
• Doubled—clubs -12; diamonds—14; hearts—16; spades—18
• Redoubled—clubs—24; diamonds—28; hearts—32; spades—36.

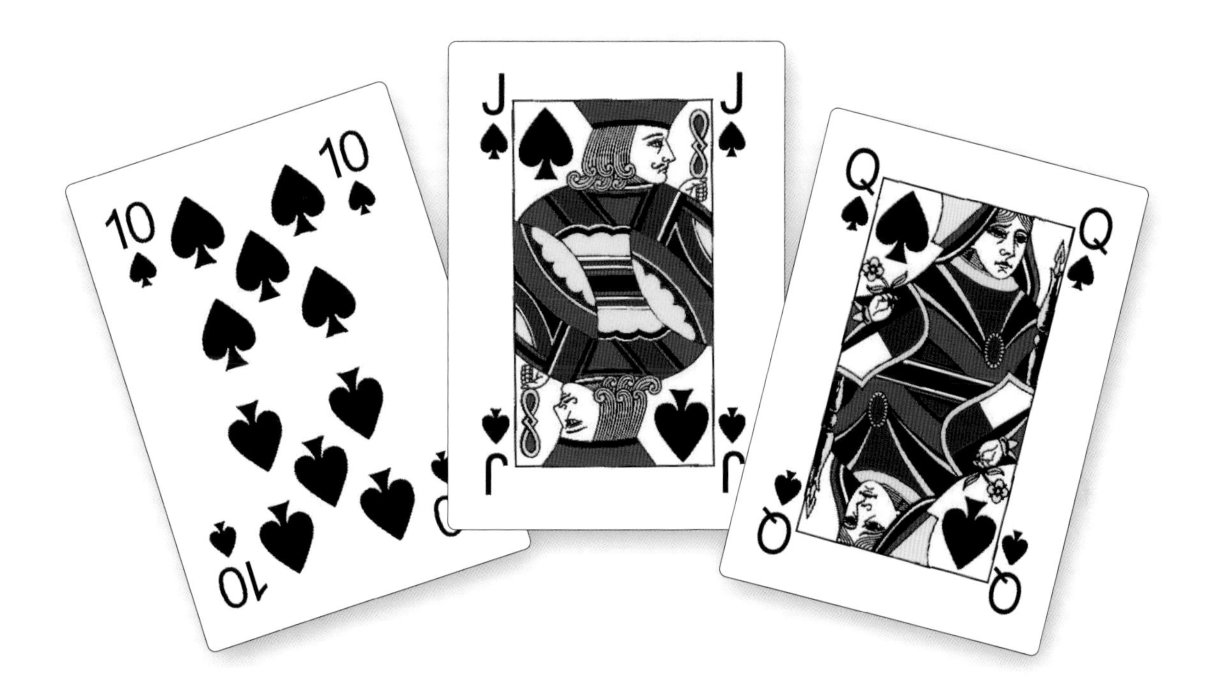

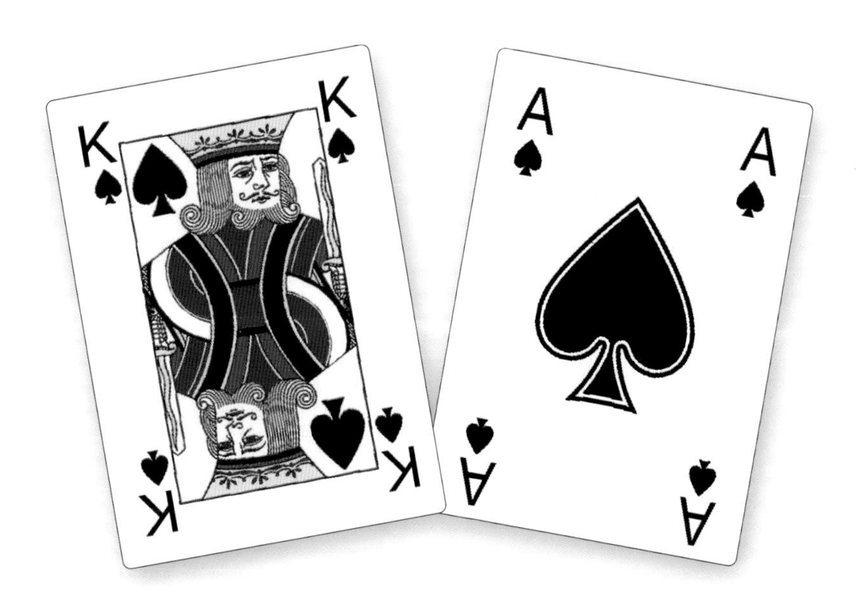

Spades are the highest suit

Other scoring disparities:

- Undertricks—scored by opponents, above the line
- Undoubled contract—50 per trick; doubled—100; redoubled—200
- Grand slam—100
- Small slam—50

Each will be above the line.

Honor cards:

- A, K, Q, J, 10 of trumps in one hand—100
- Four aces in one hand (no trumps)—100
- A, K, Q, J, 10 of trumps split between partners 4-1—90
- Any four from above in one hand—80
- A, K, Q, J, 10 of trumps split between partners 3-2—50
- Any four from above split between partners—40
- Four aces split between partners—40
- Three of the above-listed trumps in one hand—30.

The first partnership to score 30 points below the line wins the game, and the first to win two games ends the rubber and scores a bonus 250 points. Above and below the line points are then totaled up as in Contract Bridge.

THREE-HANDED BRIDGE

Four hands are dealt and one is left aside until after the bidding has finished—players bid as individuals rather than in pairs. The declarer then takes the extra hand, places it opposite himself and plays it as the dummy. Scoring is as for Contract Bridge. Each of the opponents is playing for him- or herself and, should the declarer fail to make the contract, they will each score the full number of above-the-line points. Likewise for honors and bonuses, and each player can be made vulnerable separately. Rubbers are played as the best of three, with a 2-0 score earning a bonus of 700 points and a 2-1 500.

Whist

PLAYERS: TWO TO FOUR
DECK: FULL
SCORE SHEET: YES
ACES: HIGH
ORIGIN: ENGLAND
SIMPLICITY FACTOR: 8
SKILL FACTOR: 7
SUITABLE FOR CHILDREN: 7
SUITABLE FOR GAMBLING: 6

First described by Edmund Hoyle in his 18th-century book of card games, this straightforward trumps "n" tricks game is the foundation for many other games.

In its most basic form, Whist is played with a full deck by four players in pairs, sitting opposite each other. Each is singly dealt 13 cards and the last card is turned up to signify trumps, then taken into the dealer's hand. Tricks are then played for in the conventional manner, with players following the suit led or if they can't, discarding or trumping. The winners are the

Diamonds, as trumps, wins the trick

partnership who have won the most tricks. The deal rotates to the left after each hand and scoring is optional. In this version, each pair scores one point for each trick they make over "book" (six tricks) and the winners are the first to seven points. There are, however, several variations that can make the game much more interesting.

BETTING

A cash-for-points system can be worked out.

Variations

ENGLISH WHIST

This is played the same way, but scored far more formally. Each trick over book scores one point each; winning a game scores five points; and within the taken tricks, the team holding most of the honor cards—ace, king, queen and jack of trumps—win bonus points, four points for four honors, two for three. If a team wins a game by five points to nil it wins a "treble", or three extra points; if it wins by five to one, it scores a "double", or two extra points; while a win of five to three or four is a "single", earning one extra point. The first team to win two games wins the rubber and two bonus points.

GERMAN WHIST

This version is played with two players, who start with 13 cards each from a full deck and the next one is turned up for trumps. Once the first trick is won (they are played for as in basic Whist) the winner picks up the turned up card and the loser takes the face-down one beneath it and the next card is turned up. The winner of the previous trick leads and the procedure with the pack is repeated until the pack is exhausted. The remaining tricks are then played out and the winner is the one with the most tricks. This version is ideal for gambling, as the loser can pay the winner a pre-agreed sum for each trick his total is short of his opponent's.

BID WHIST

Bid Whist is played by two teams of two, but the trumps are bid for as players nominate the number of tricks they think they can make plus the number of honor cards they believe they can finish up with. One point is awarded for each trick and the honor cards are scored as one point for each. Scores are cumulative, and if the successful bidder makes the contract, they score the difference between their total and their opponents', while if they fail to make contract, they score nothing and the other side gets their full score.

KNOCKOUT WHIST

This can be played by up to seven players, and seven cards are dealt to each with the next card turned up to signify trumps. It is played as the basic game, except any player who doesn't make a single trick in a hand is "knocked out" to take no further part in the game and the winner is the last player left in. The game could be won in the first hand if a player takes all seven tricks.

Scotch Whist

PLAYERS: THREE TO SEVEN

DECK: NOTHING BELOW A SIX

SCORE SHEET: YES

ACES: HIGH

ORIGIN: NOT SCOTLAND!

SIMPLICITY FACTOR: 8

SKILL FACTOR: 8

SUITABLE FOR CHILDREN: 7

SUITABLE FOR GAMBLING: 6

This isn't really Whist as the tricks taken don't count for anything, and it's probably safe to assume that it isn't from Scotland either. But it is a fun, fast-moving game in which the idea is to capture certain cards.

Although it can be played by different numbers, the classic form has two teams of two seated opposite each other, with a pack that has every card below the six removed. In the trumps suit the highest ranked card is the jack. Each player is dealt nine cards, with the final one being turned up as trumps then taken into the dealer's hand. The number of tricks taken by each pair isn't important, it's what's in the tricks that count. The winners are the pair who gets to 41 points first.

Jacks high

SCORING

Teams score the following points for finishing up with certain trump cards: the jack—11 points; the ace—4, the king—3; the queen—2; the ten—10. They also score one point for each card over ten (half the pack) they finish up with.

Variations

When played with six people (when, confusingly, it is sometimes called French Whist) they are in three teams of two, but if it involves three, five or seven players, they all play individually. With three players they have 12 cards each; with five they have seven; and seven they have five cards. Odd cards can be used to signify trumps but are of no other use, and points scored for counting cards are awarded one for every card a player finishes up with over the number he started with.

Did you know?

Scotch Whist is a variation on Whist and it is unclear how it came by its name. It is one of many games that is difficult to pin down, and debates would probably rage long and hard about how the game should be played. There are many versions of the classic game of Whist and many of them are named after different countries—Romanian, Israeli and German to name but a few. However, these names are probably more about trying to distinguish the different versions, than about the games having any particular link with the country!

Whist was widely played in the 18th and 19th centuries, and is thought to be descended from a 17th century game called Ruffs and Honors. The beauty of the family of Whist games is that they are usually easy to learn in the first place, but they then take time and concentration to master them completely, so they are never dull.

JOKER

CHAPTER 2

Children's and Party Games

This collection includes a perfect mix of old favorites and, hopefully, some you haven't played before, from simple games of chance and memory for the youngest children such as Snap and Concentration, to more boisterous competitive games for older players such as Racing Demon and Cheat! If you're looking for a simple betting game, turn to Hoggenheimer, and if you're looking for an introduction to Poker, Brag is your game.

Animals

PLAYERS: THE MORE THE MERRIER
DECK: COULD BE SEVERAL
SCORE SHEET: NO
ACES: HIGH
ORIGIN: GERMANY
SIMPLICITY FACTOR: 10
SKILL FACTOR: 4
SUITABLE FOR CHILDREN: 10

An excellent, if rather noisy game for children, Animals can be highly entertaining for adults who've been in the bar all evening! In theory it can be played with two players, but the fun factor increases as the numbers go up. If the numbers get above half a dozen or so, multiple packs should be used.

Each player assumes the name of an animal of their choice, if necessary the packs are shuffled together and all the cards are dealt out face-down. In turn, each player turns over the top card of his pile to make a new face-up pile in front of them. This continues until two matching cards are turned over, at which point each player involved has to shout the other's animal name. The first to do so captures the other player's face-up pile. When all a player's cards are gone, they drop out and the winner is the one who finishes up with all the cards.

Variations

It's always amusing for players to have to make a rival's animal noise instead of merely shouting the name.

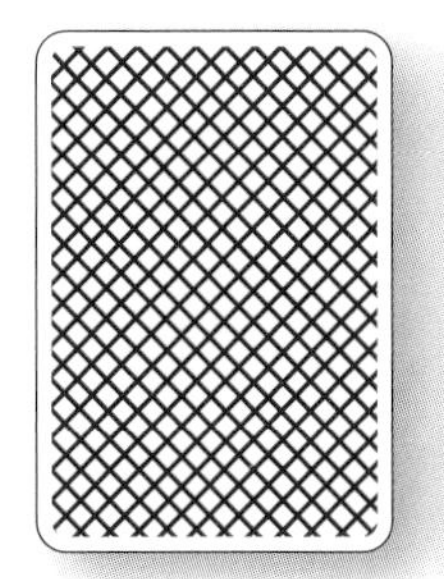

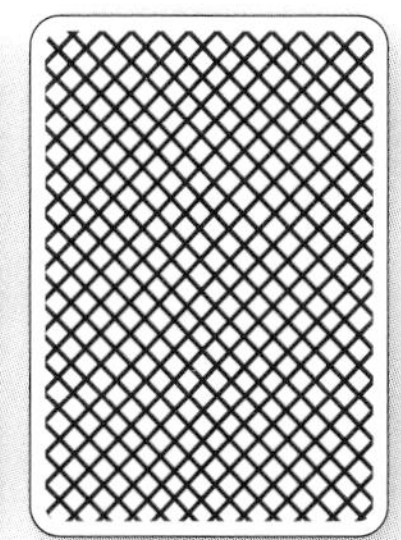

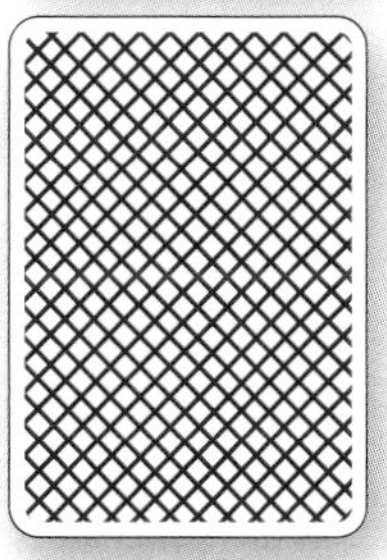

Beat Your Neighbor

PLAYERS: ANY

DECK: FULL

SCORE SHEET: NO

ACES: HIGH

ORIGIN: GERMANY

SIMPLICITY FACTOR: 9

SKILL FACTOR: 7 (IF GAMBLING)

SUITABLE FOR CHILDREN: 8

SUITABLE FOR GAMBLING: 9

In spite of its less-than-glamorous name, this game is actually quite a close relative of Stud Poker. But think how it would have sounded if, in the classic poker film *The Cincinnatti Kid*, Steve McQueen had sat across the green baize with Edward G Robinson to play a game called Beat Your Neighbor!

Each of any number of players is dealt, singly, five cards that remain face-down in front of them. The first player turns over his top card, the player to his left turns over his cards until he beats the first player either with a higher card or a pair. As soon as he does this, he stops and the next player continues trying to beat what the second one has, and so on. If a player turns all of his cards without beating the previous player, then he must drop out. Once everybody has had a turn, the first player continues to try to beat the last. This continues until only one player is left.

BETTING

Players can bet up to a prescribed limit after each turn of their cards, wagering that their neighbor will not be able to beat them. The bets go into a pot that is collected by the winner.

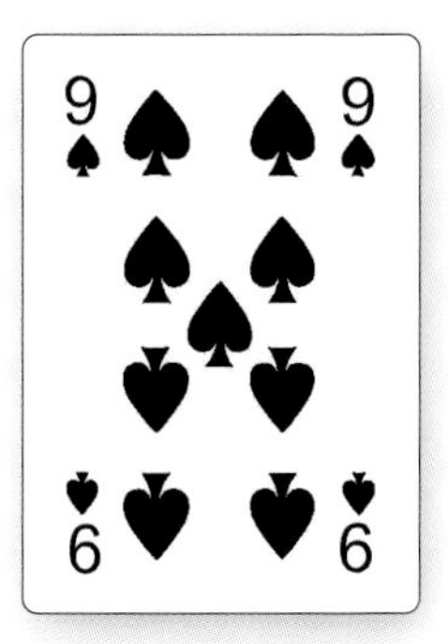

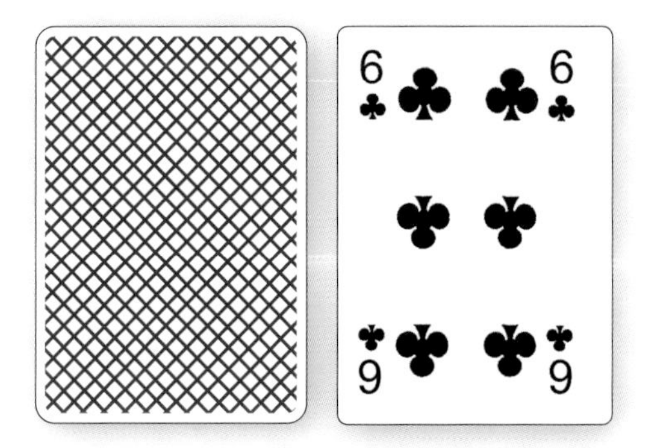

The top card wins

Slap Jack

PLAYERS: THREE OR MORE

DECK: FULL

SCORE SHEET: NO

ACES: HIGH

ORIGIN: ENGLAND

SIMPLICITY FACTOR: 10

SKILL FACTOR: 4

SUITABLE FOR CHILDREN: 10

This is a good game for young children because it is very simple to play, and it is one of the more physical card games.

A dealer is chosen and the cards are shuffled. The cards are dealt out face-down into piles in front of each player. If there are more than 10 players, more than one pack can be used. Once each player has a pile of cards in front of him, the fun can begin!

On a signal from the dealer, each player turns a card from his pile and places it in the centre of the table. Cards are then turned up in this way until a Jack is played. As soon as a Jack is revealed the race is on to be the first one to slap their hand down on the Jack. The first player to slap the Jack, takes the Jack and all the cards underneath it. These cards are then put at the bottom of the players pile.

The jack-slapping continues until one player has won all the cards and so wins the game.

If a player has no more cards he can stay in the game until the next Jack is played. If he can slap that Jack first, he can stay in the game. If he fails, he is out of the game completely.

When more than one player slaps at a Jack, it is the player whose hand is lowest in the heap of hands, or directly on top of the Jack, that wins the pile.

If a player slaps any card that is not a jack, he must give one card, face down, to the player who put the card down.

Snap!

PLAYERS: MORE THAN TWO

DECK: FULL

SIMPLICITY FACTOR: 10

SKILL FACTOR: 2

SUITABLE FOR CHILDREN: 9

The ultimate children's card game and probably everybody's first experience of playing cards. It hasn't changed at all over the years, or should that be centuries?

A full deck of cards is dealt out face-down in piles in front of each player—more than one deck can be shuffled together if there are many players. In rotation to the left, players turn over their top card on to the pile in the centre. When two cards of the same value are turned up simultaneously, the players all shout "Snap!". The first one to do so collects the pile in the centre, turns it upside down and puts it on the bottom of their own pile. The winner is the one to collect all the cards.

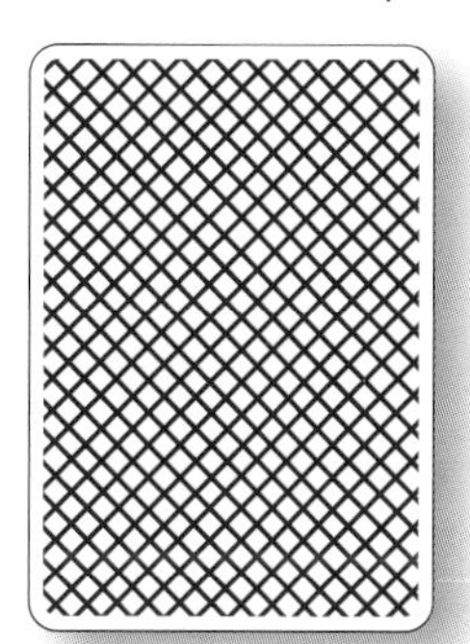

A slight variation is for the players to each make their own piles of upturned cards, again turning them over in rotation. When the cards on two piles match and "Snap!" is called, the winner wins those two piles only.

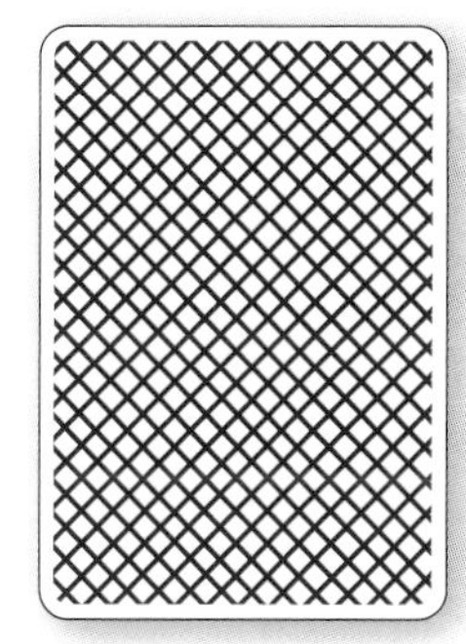

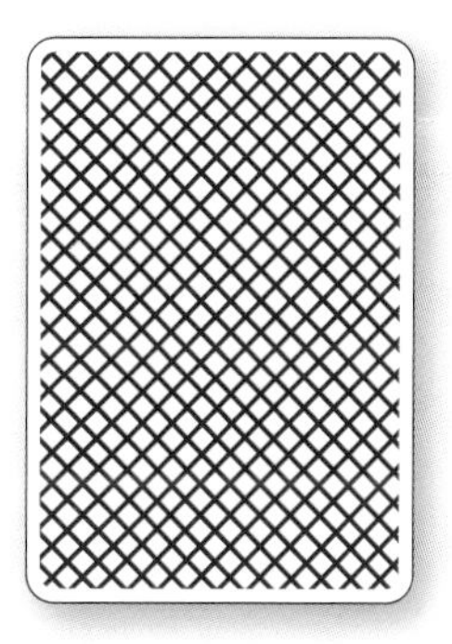

Snap!

Racing Demon

PLAYERS: THREE TO TEN

DECK: ONE DECK PER PERSON (EACH PACK MUST BE DISTINCTIVE)

SCORE SHEET: YES

SIMPLICITY FACTOR: 4

SKILL FACTOR: 2

SUITABLE FOR CHILDREN: 5

Also known as Demon, Nerts, Squeal and Speed this highly-competitive game is a fast-moving variation of Patience. As the names suggest, the secret of success is ruthlessness and speed! You'll need a big playing area, a large table preferably. Each player takes the jokers from their deck and shuffles them. Then, on a signal, the decks are passed to the player on the left, and the race begins!

Each player counts out thirteen cards as quickly as they can and puts them down in front of them, with the top card face up. Then they put four cards, face up, beside this.

The main aim is to get rid of the pile of thirteen cards, so if the top card is an ace this is put out in the middle, and the next card is turned up.

If one of the four cards is an ace, this is put out in the middle and the top card from the pile of thirteen is used to fill the gap. The next card on the pile is turned over. The top card from your pile of thirteen can be added to the set of four cards. If you have a red queen, a black jack can be added, then a red ten and so on.

If players have no playable cards in front of them, they can also turn the rest of the pack over three at a time, and put the top cards out in the middle if they can find a home for them.

The aces in the middle are there for everyone to build on, so play needs to be quick! The aces must be built on in strict order: Ace of hearts, two of hearts and on until the king of hearts which is placed face down to show it is complete. Play continues until one player has put out all thirteen cards, and shouts: STOP!

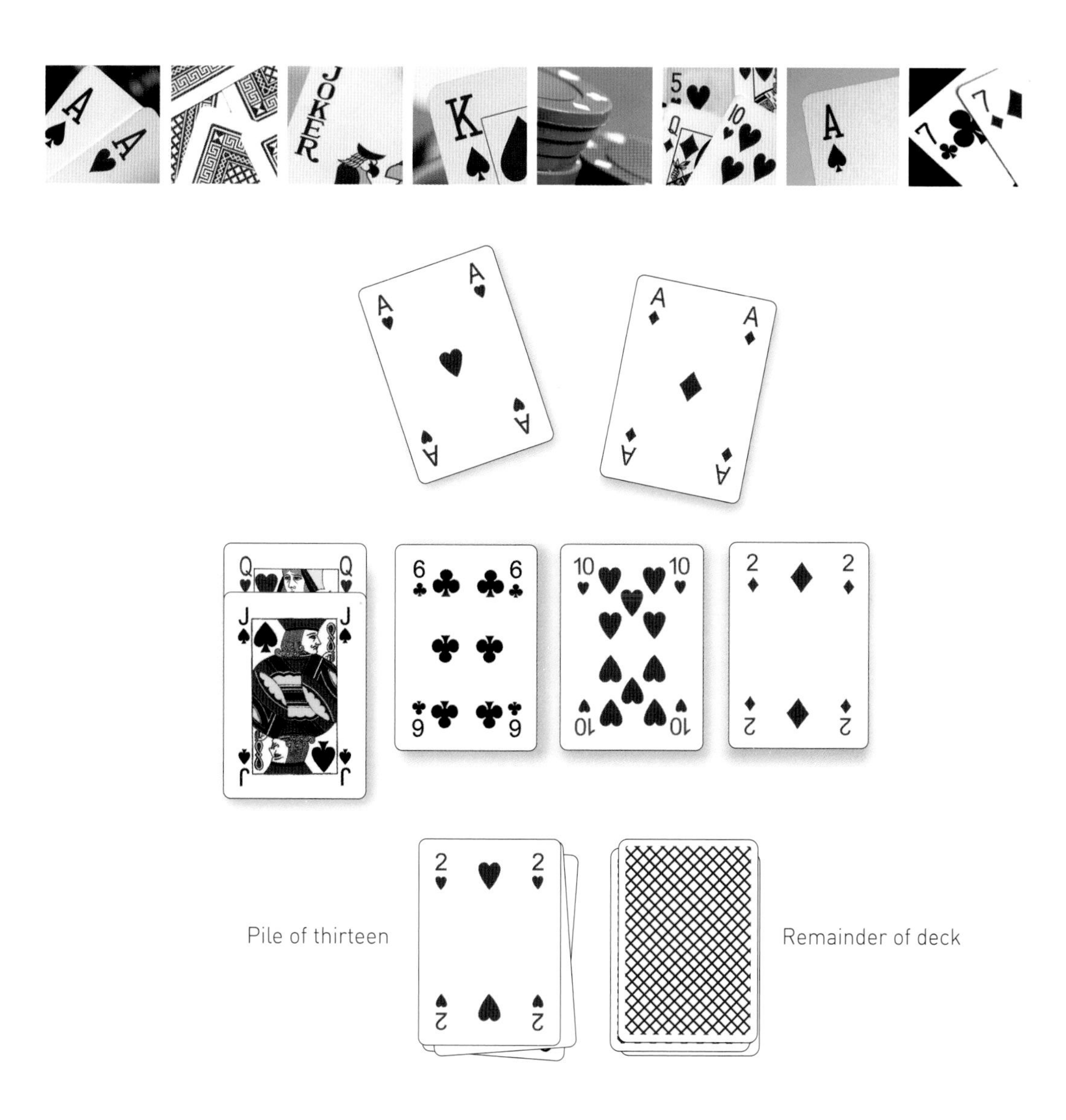

The other players count how many cards they have left in their pile of thirteen. Then all the cards in the middle are gathered up and sorted into packs. This can take quite a while if there are lots of people playing, but excitement builds as each player sees how many cards, or how few, he has managed to get out!

Each player then counts their cards from the middle, and subtracts the number left in their pile of thirteen. Each players' score is noted on a score sheet, the cards are shuffled and passed, and play begins again. The player with the lowest score at the end of an agreed number of games is the winner.

It's a complex game to grasp, but once you have mastered the basics you'll find it addictive!

Hoggenheimer

PLAYERS: TWO TO TEN

DECK: A PIQUET PACK, 32 CARDS FROM ACE TO 7, AND ONE OTHER CARD, USUALLY THE 2 OF CLUBS.

SCORE SHEET: NO

ACES: HIGH

SIMPLICITY FACTOR: 2

SKILL FACTOR: 1

SUITABLE FOR CHILDREN: 7

SUITABLE FOR GAMBLING: 10

This simple game of chance can be played for any stakes. Players take turns to be the banker. The cards are shuffled, and cut by the player on the banker's left. Then the banker deals out the 32 cards, face down, in four rows of eight. The thirty-third card is put face down beside the grid.

To start play, the banker turns the extra card, and this is put in its correct place in the grid. The card it replaces is put in its correct place and so on, until the 2 of clubs turns up. If the card you have bet on is turned over, you win.

Each player chooses a card or cards, and puts their stake down. A player selects a pair of cards or an entire row or column, by placing a counter touching two cards to show a pair, or at the top of a column or beside a row. But, you only get your stake back if all the cards in your stake are turned over. If you bet on one card, you get one counter back. If you bet on 2, you win 2 counters. If you bet on a row of 8, you win 8 counters.

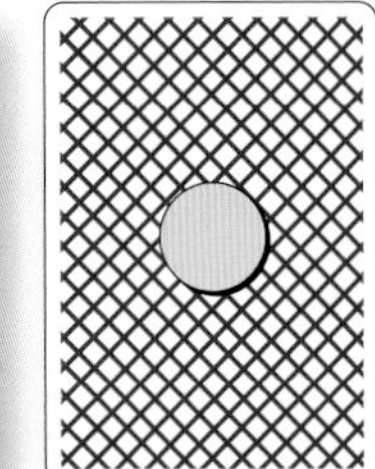

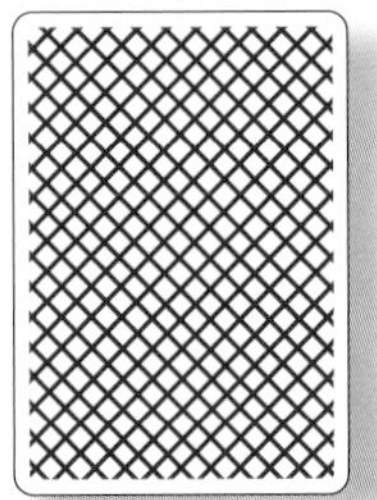

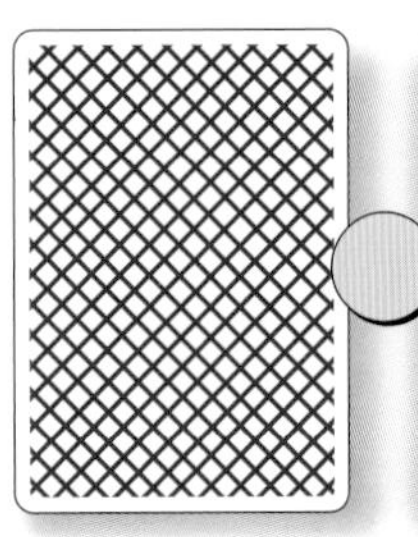

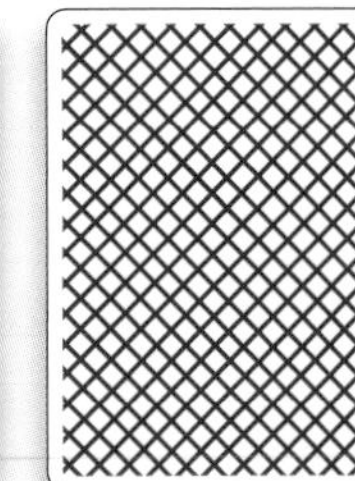

If the extra card is the two of clubs, this means the banker wins, and he takes all the stake money! And the bank passes to the next player. Sometimes the two of clubs is the last card to show up and then the banker pays everybody.

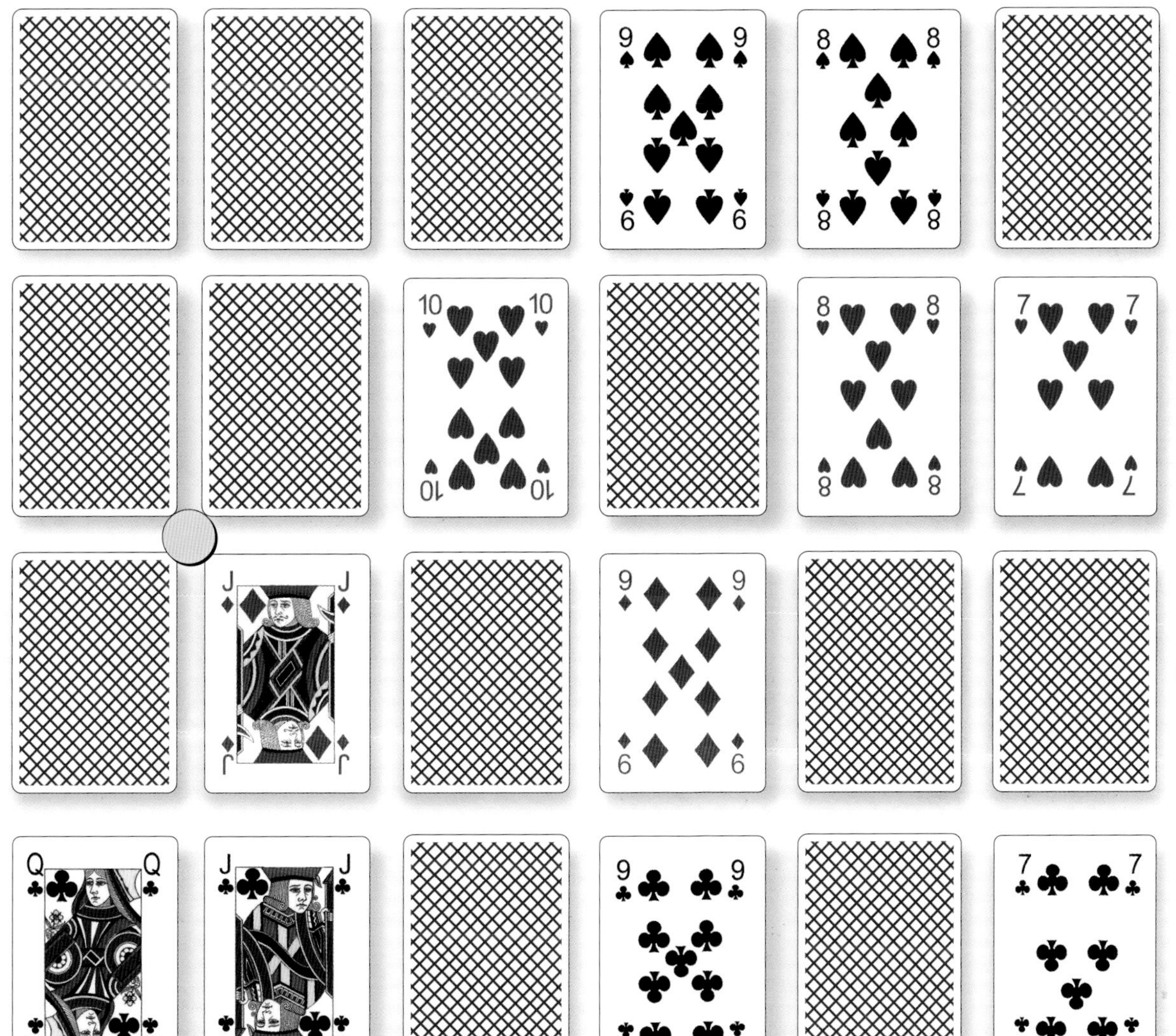

My Ship Sails

PLAYERS: FOUR OR MORE

SCORE SHEET: NO

DECK: ONE FULL DECK FOR EVERY SIX PLAYERS

SIMPLICITY FACTOR: 10

SKILL FACTOR: 6

SUITABLE FOR CHILDREN: 10

SUITABLE FOR GAMBLING: 0

To get the maximum enjoyment out of this game, the trick is to play it quickly, so players have to make their minds up and make their moves within a very short time limit. When played like that, it's a fantastic game for children as it's easy to understand yet enjoys a high excitement factor.

Ideally, there should be half a dozen players, though it can be played with any number over three. If more than six are taking part, then two packs should be shuffled together.

A full deck is shuffled and seven cards are dealt to each player. The object is to collect seven cards in a single suit but of any denomination. To do this, the players select one discard from their hand and place it face-down on the table in front of them. Then everybody slides their discarded card to the player on the left and picks up the card that has been slid in front of them. This process is repeated until one player has all seven cards of the same suit, calls "My ship sails" and wins the game. Often, the suit the winner finishes up with will not be the one he started out collecting, so it's not a good idea to be too inflexible.

Someone's ship sails

Last In

PLAYERS: FOUR TO SIX

DECK: FULL

SCORE SHEET: NO

ACES: HIGH

SIMPLICITY FACTOR: 9

SKILL FACTOR: 3

SUITABLE FOR CHILDREN: 10

SUITABLE FOR GAMBLING: 0

An interesting variation of the standard trumps "n" trick-winning game, for between four and six players.

Using a full deck, six cards are dealt for four players, five for five players and four for six players. The last card dealt—to the dealer—will be shown to the other players before the dealer takes it into his hand. The remaining cards are put into a stack in the middle of the table.

Tricks are played for as normal, but before leading the next trick, the winner of each trick takes the top card from the stack and absorbs it into his hand without making a discard. This means that some players will have more cards than others. As soon as all a player's cards are played he drops out, and the winner is the last man left in. If two players are left with one card each to contest a hand's final trick, the winner of the game is whichever one takes that trick.

BETTING

Last In isn't really a gambler's game, so the best way to wager is for each player to put into a pot at the beginning of each hand and the winner takes all.

Cheat!

PLAYERS: THREE TO TEN

DECK: FULL

SIMPLICITY FACTOR: 4

SKILL FACTOR: 2

SUITABLE FOR CHILDREN: 7

The dealer deals the deck out equally among the players. Any odd cards are put in a discard pile in the middle of the table. All the players have a few minutes to look at and sort their cards. Then play begins on the dealer's left.

The first player puts a card face down on the discard pile (if there is one), saying the number of card out loud as he puts it down, let's say it's a six. Then the next player must follow by putting down a seven, again saying the number as he does so. If the next player doesn't have a seven, he can put down any other card. As the card is put down on the pile, if any player thinks they are lying, they shout: "Cheat!" and the player who put down the card must turn it over to show what it is. If it was a cheat, they must pick up the discard pile. If it was true, the player who called "cheat" must pick up the cards. The player to the left of the "cheat" can then start play again with the card of their choice. Play goes on like this, following in number sequence 9, 10, Jack, Queen, King, Ace, then 2, 3, 4, 5, 6, 7, 8 and so on.

The first player to put down all their cards is the winner.

Variations

Players can also try to put down more than one card without being spotted!

Go Fish

PLAYERS: TWO TO FIVE

DECK: FULL

SCORE SHEET: NO

ORIGIN: USA

SIMPLICITY FACTOR: 8

SKILL FACTOR: 6

SUITABLE FOR CHILDREN: 10

This is an entertaining game from the U.S. for two to five players that relies on cunning and memory as much as traditional card game skills. Five cards are dealt per player if there are four or five players and seven if there are two or three. The remainder are put face-down in the centre as a pot.

The idea is to make "books"—sets of four cards of a similar value—by asking fellow players for particular cards. To start, the player to the left of the dealer can ask any other player in the game for particular cards, saying "give me your sevens" (or whatever). The player asked must hand them over if he has them and the player who asked has another go. If he hasn't he tells him to "Go Fish!" and the player who asked must take the top card off the pot. If this is of the value he demanded or is the final card needed to make any book (not just of the value he was asking for) he can take another turn and once again ask any player for any cards. If not, he places the card in his hand and the player on his left takes a turn.

Books made are placed on the table in front of each player and the winner is the first player to have put all his cards down in books, which ends the game.

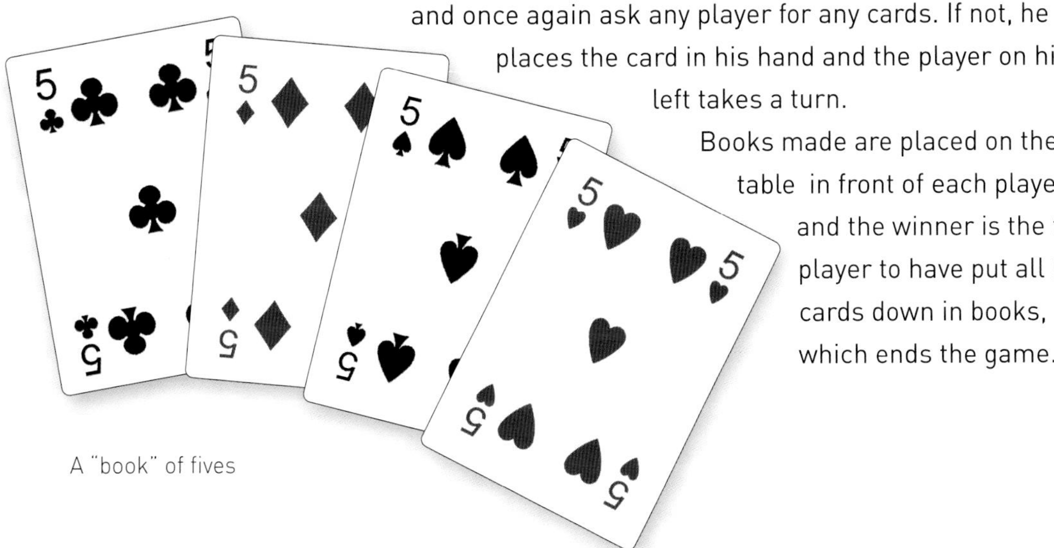

A "book" of fives

Good Morning Jack

PLAYERS: ANY

DECK: SEVERAL

ORIGIN: USA

SIMPLICITY FACTOR: 9

SKILL FACTOR: 3

SUITABLE FOR CHILDREN: 10

Good Morning Jack has such an enormous potential for downright silliness that, while it is essentially a fast-moving game that can give children a great deal of fun, it also has an almost unlimited after-bar appeal.

There can be any number of players, but if it gets to be more than about five, it's best to use more than one deck of cards shuffled together. All the cards are dealt out face-down in front of each player. The first player leads by turning his top card up in the middle of the table, the next player does the same, putting his on top of the first and so on around the table. There are a number of "score cards". When they are turned up, every player must perform a prescribed action and the last to do so takes the pile in the middle and adds it, face-down, to the bottom of his pile. If a king is turned up the players must salute the king—literally. If it's a queen they must bow to the queen. They have to say "Good Morning Jack" to a jack and knock on the table for a seven.

The fun starts as the pace gets quicker and the players more careless and carelessly anticipatory. To spice things up, other actions can be added for any of the other cards—stand up for the two; pull your left ear for the five; stand up and turn around for the ten and so on. The winner is the first player to get rid of all his cards, but on playing his last one he must say "Last card". If he doesn't, he takes the pot and the game continues.

Old Maid

PLAYERS: THREE OR MORE

DECK: FULL

SCORE SHEET: NO

ORIGIN: FRANCE

SIMPLICITY FACTOR: 10

SKILL FACTOR: 4

SUITABLE FOR CHILDREN: 8

A classic children's card game, Old Maid originated several hundred years ago in France, where it was called "Le Vieux Garçon" (The Old Boy).

First one queen is removed from a full deck (in the French version it will be a jack) and all the remaining 51 cards are dealt out to the players. It doesn't matter if they aren't holding exactly the same number of cards each. The players look at their hands and sort them out into numerical pairs, which are put on the table in front of them. If a player holds three of a kind, a pair is put down but the remaining card is held on to. Four of a kind are put down as two pairs. The player to the left of the dealer then turns to the player on their left and offers their hand so the other player can take a card without seeing what it is. If this card makes a pair it is put down, if it doesn't it is absorbed into their hand. That player then turns to the player on his left and the process is repeated.

This continues until all the cards have been laid out in pairs and one player is left holding the odd queen. That player has lost and the others make the most of calling him or her an "Old Maid". (Or when playing in France, a "Vieux Garçon".)

Eights

PLAYERS: TWO TO SIX

DECK: FULL

SCORE SHEET: YES

ACES: LOW

ORIGIN: GERMANY

SIMPLICITY FACTOR: 8

SKILL FACTOR: 7

SUITABLE FOR CHILDREN: 9

SUITABLE FOR GAMBLING: 6

A fast-moving game that is sometimes known as Stops, Eights can be played with two to six players.

If the game is for two, three or four players, seven cards are dealt to each, if five or six players, five cards. The top card of the remainder is turned up and placed next to it. The player to start has to cover this with a card of the same value or same suit from his hand. If he can't, he draws cards from the pot (the pile of remaining cards) until he can, and the game continues. All four eights are "wild" and can be played at any time and nominated as any suit, which then has to be followed by the next player in turn. For example, the eight of hearts could be played on top of the queen of spades, and clubs be declared, so the next player has to follow with a club.

Avoid the eights!

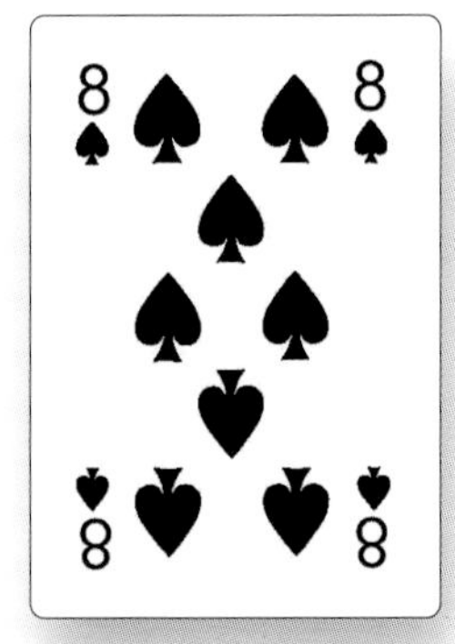

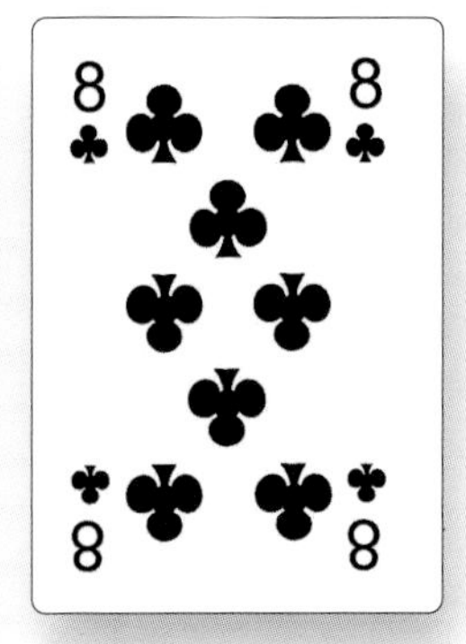

The winner is the first player to get rid of all his cards, and scores points from the others relative to the value of the cards they are still holding. If play is stopped as no player can go, the values of each player's hand is counted and the winner is the one with the lowest score.

SCORING

When the players' hands have to be counted, each eight scores 50 points, picture cards 10 each and the others score their face value with an ace counting as one.

BETTING

A simple points-for-cash system is advised, with the losing players each paying the winner the value of their hands.

Did you know?

Eights belongs to a family of games where play consists of matching the rank or suit of the previous card laid down. There are often certain cards that are given special qualities that can be used in play. Because the structure of the game is so simple it has been easy for players to build on and to adapt the game, adding extra rules and elements without upsetting the overall balance. There are a few commercial card games that have been developed that are based on Eights, and are played with special packs of cards. The most famous of these is Uno.

War

PLAYERS: TWO OR MORE

DECK: FULL

SCORE SHEET: NO

SIMPLICITY FACTOR: 10

SKILL FACTOR: 0

SUITABLE FOR CHILDREN: 8

An exciting kids' game for two or more players (here the two-handed version is explained). War is sometimes called Everlasting due to the length of time a game can take, it is ideal for long journeys or rainy holidays.

A full deck is dealt out into two face-down piles, one in front of each player. They each turn their top card over on to the table side by side. Whoever plays the numerically highest card, regardless of suit, wins both cards and puts them, face-down, on the bottom of their pile. Should they both be of equal value, the players must "go to war", which means they each play a card face-down next to their original tied card, they then play another card face-up on top of it and the highest card takes all six. If those cards tie also, then the war goes on—another card is played face-down before the next one is played face-up. This will continue until there is a winner from the face-up cards and that player takes all the cards in the centre, which are sorted to face-down and put on the bottom of his pile.

The game continues until one player wins by taking all the cards. Or one of the players dies of old age!

Variations

The game can be played with more players and more than one deck, but cards left over from the deal should be removed so that all the hands are equal. It is played exactly

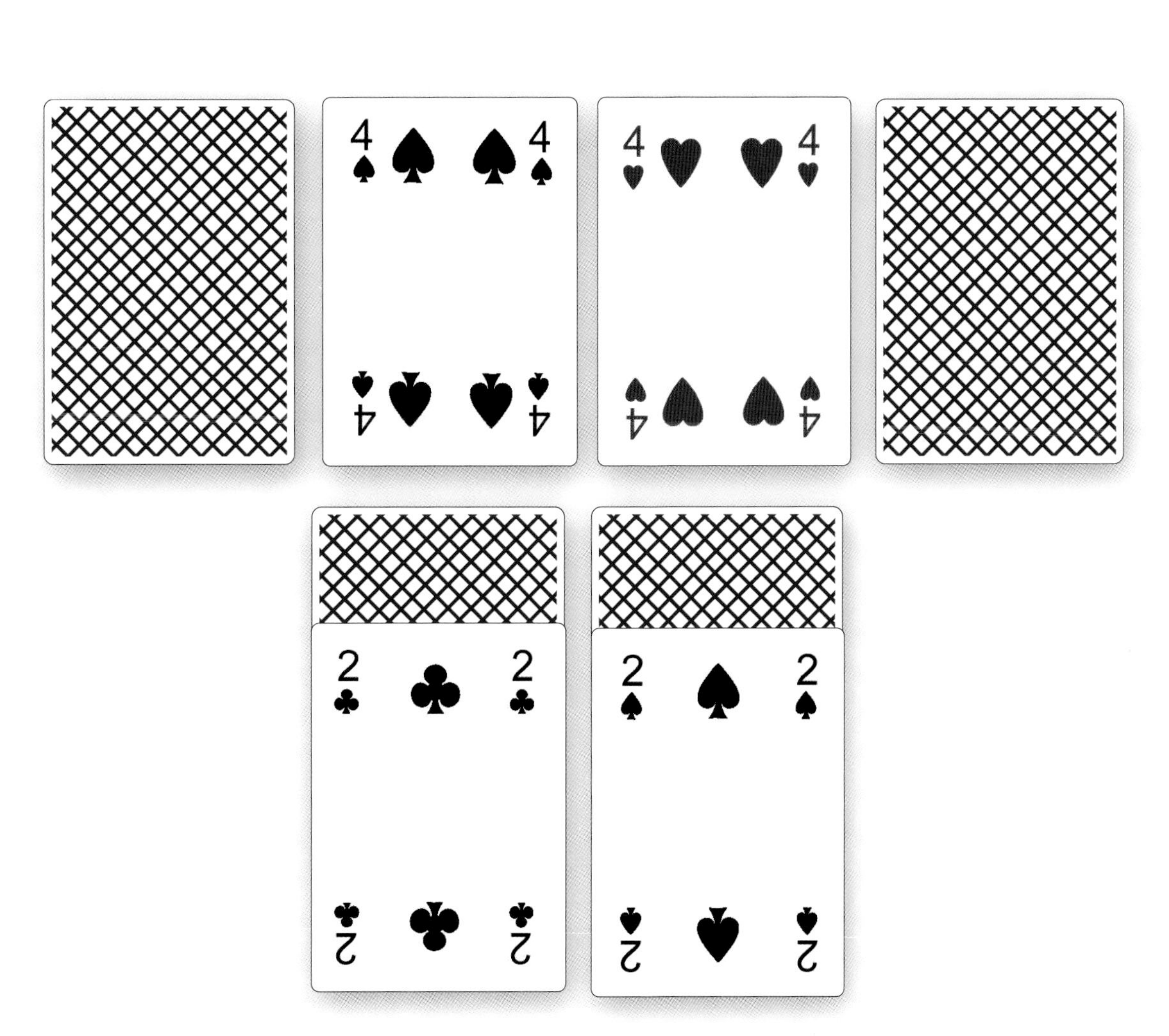

Going to war

as before, with the winner taking all the cards in the centre, and when the winning cards are part of a tie, then all the players join in the war that is again played out until somebody wins it. Once a player loses all of his cards, he drops out and the rest carry on until there is a clear winner.

Snip Snap Snorem

PLAYERS: THREE TO EIGHT

DECK: FULL

SCORE SHEET: NO

ORIGIN: ENGLAND

SIMPLICITY FACTOR: 8

SKILL FACTOR: 6

SUITABLE FOR CHILDREN: 10

SUITABLE FOR GAMBLING: 7

If played at speed, this fairly rowdy stopping game is one that younger children are guaranteed to enjoy.

All the cards in a full deck are dealt out to the players, who can number between three and eight. If any cards are left over, the top one is turned over as a starter, if not then the player on the dealer's left starts by playing any card from his hand. The next player round to have a card of the same numerical value plays it on top and says "Snip", the next player with a card of that value plays it on top and declares "Snap" and the player with the final card of that denomination plays it to call "Snorem". Any players who haven't got a card of that value miss a turn, and the player who called "Snorem" starts things off again with a card of any denomination he chooses.

The winner is the first player to get rid of all his cards. As players can look at their hands there are more tactics involved in this game than you might at first think!

BETTING

Chips can be paid to the winner by the losers at the rate of one per card held when the game stops.

"Snip!"... "Snap!"... "Snorem!"

Variations

JIG

Instead of playing cards of the same numerical value, cards are played in same suit sequence, up or down, so the seven of spades would be followed by either the eight or the six. The sequence would then continue in that direction for four cards only until the player who called "Snorem" starts another sequence.

EARL OF COVENTRY

The same as Snip Snap Snorem except the lead player, if he played a four, would call "That's as good as four can be". The next player to play a four would say "There's a four as good as he". The third continues with "There's the best of all the three", while the fourth player would finish the rhyme off with "And there's the Earl of Coventry!"

Stealing The Old Man's Bundle

PLAYERS: TWO TO FOUR

DECK: FULL

SCORE SHEET: NO

SIMPLICITY FACTOR: 6

SKILL FACTOR: 7

SUITABLE FOR CHILDREN: 10

An entertaining children's game, for between two and four players, that requires a little more thought than most.

Each player is singly dealt four cards and four cards are put face-up in the middle of the table. Going in rotation to the left from the dealer, if a player can numerically—or picture for picture—match any card in the centre with one in his hand, he takes the card from the centre and puts it face-up with his own card near him on the table. It is his "bundle". If he can match more than one with the same card he will take them all into his bundle, or, if a card in his hand matches the top card on another player's bundle, when it is his turn he can take that whole bundle. If he has no matches in his hand he must put a card from his hand face-up in the row in the centre, which is called "trailing".

After all players have played all their cards, each is dealt another four, with no more being put into the centre. When all the cards are played out, the winner is the one with the most cards in front of them, in other words, the biggest bundle.

Fan Tan

PLAYERS: THREE TO EIGHT

DECK: FULL

SCORE SHEET: NO

ACES: LOW

SIMPLICITY FACTOR: 9

SKILL FACTOR: 5

SUITABLE FOR CHILDREN: 8

SUITABLE FOR GAMBLING: 10

Played with three to eight players, Fan Tan is a cousin of Eights but is less complicated and far more suitable for gambling.

All the cards are dealt and the player to the dealer's left has to play any seven. If he hasn't got one he puts a chip into the pot and the player to his left has to play one. If he can't the same thing happens, but if he can, the player to his left has to follow suit with either the six or the eight and the next player has to follow with, depending on what was played, the five or the nine. This goes up or down to the king or the ace respectively, with any player who can't follow putting a chip into the pot before the next player tries. Once a suit has run out, another seven has to be played and the process is repeated. The winner is the player who gets rid of all his cards first. He takes the pot and one chip for every card in the hands of each of the other players.

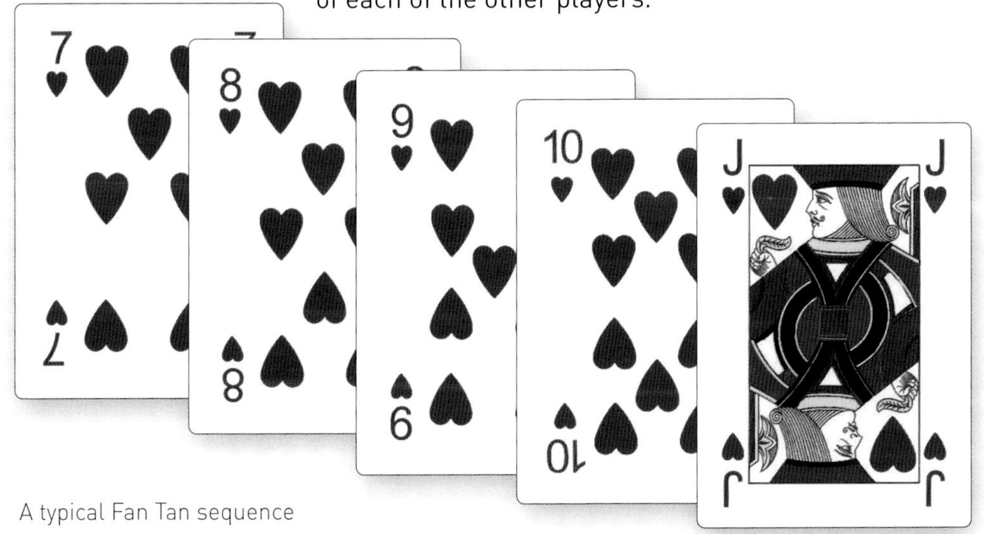

A typical Fan Tan sequence

Go Boom!

PLAYERS: TWO TO SIX

DECK: FULL

SCORE SHEET: NO (UNLESS THE GAME IS BEING SCORED)

ACES: HIGH

ORIGIN: USA

SIMPLICITY FACTOR: 9

SKILL FACTOR: 3

SUITABLE FOR CHILDREN: 10

A very simple game for between two and six players, Go Boom! is particularly suitable for young children as a step up from Snap!

Seven cards are dealt to each player and the remainder makes up a face-down pot. The player to the left of the dealer leads. The other players must match that card either by face value or suit. For example, the queen of hearts could be followed by any heart card or any other queen. The winner of the trick is whoever played the highest card in the suit that was led.

If any player can't follow either suit or value they must draw cards from the pot, until they can either follow suit or value or have taken three cards. The winner is the first player to get rid of all the cards in their hand. The only advantage of winning tricks is that the winner leads for the next trick, otherwise they don't count for anything. The winner will announce his victory by shouting "Boom!" as he plays his last card.

SCORING

As a rule, games of Go Boom! are not scored as that tends to slow the pace down, but there is a system which can be put in place. Once a game has been won, the cards each player is left holding are totted up and added to a running total on a score sheet. Aces count for 11, picture cards 10, and everything else at face value. Once one player has reached a prearranged score, the game ends and the overall winner is whoever has the lowest score.

Chase the Ace

PLAYERS: THREE TO TEN

DECK: FULL

SCORE SHEET: NO

ACES: LOW

SIMPLICITY FACTOR: 8

SKILL FACTOR: 2

SUITABLE FOR CHILDREN: 8

Each player needs three counters. And the aim of the game is to avoid being the player with the lowest card—ace being the lowest.

The dealer deals one card to each player and puts the rest of the deck on the table. The player to the left of the dealer looks at his card first. If it is a king he places it face up in front on him. Otherwise, he can choose to "stick" if he has a fairly high card, or he can pass his low card on the player to his left. The play continues around the table as each player decides to stick or pass, until play returns to the dealer. The dealer turns over his card, and can either stick or take a new card from the pack. Once the dealer has played, all the cards are revealed and the player with the lowest card hands in a counter to show he has lost a life. The deal passes round the table to the left.

If at the end of play two players hold the same low card, the suits are ranked from lowest to highest as clubs, diamonds, hearts and spades.

Clubs are lowest, spades are highest

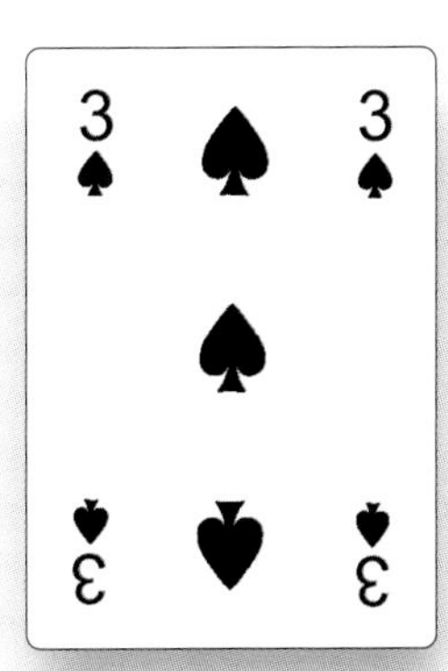

Donkey

PLAYERS: UP TO THIRTEEN

SCORE SHEET: YES

DECK: VARIES ACCORDING TO THE NUMBER OF PLAYERS

SIMPLICITY FACTOR: 10

SKILL FACTOR: 7

SUITABLE FOR CHILDREN: 10

A children's game that can be of enormous amusement value for adults, especially after a few drinks!

Up to 13 players can play and the pack will be adjusted accordingly, with one set of four same-value cards being used per player. These can be any sets, as the game concerns their similarity not their face value. Each player is dealt four cards. Simultaneously, each player passes a card of his choice to the player on his left. The process is repeated until a player has four cards the same. When they do, they lay their hand down and make a pre-arranged signal, which can be as silly as you like—braying like a donkey is a favorite, or standing on your chair. On this sign, the other players must do the same thing and the last to do so loses, making them the donkey.

Variations

There are many possible ways of scoring for Donkey. In one variation, each player has a set of letters to spell the word Donkey. And each time a player loses a life they put out a letter at a time, the first person to spell out the word Donkey is the overall loser.

Donkey is sometimes known as Pig! In this game, the first player with a set of four cards places their finger on their nose, the last person to do the same is the Pig, and out of the game.

Another variation is called Spoons. In this version a pile of spoons are put in the middle of the playing area (one less spoon than there are players), and when a player gets four cards they grab a spoon. All the other players then scramble to grab a spoon too. The player who doesn't get a spoon is out.

Ninety-Nine!

PLAYERS: TWO TO EIGHT	
DECK: FULL	
SCORE SHEET: YES	
SIMPLICITY FACTOR: 9	
SKILL FACTOR: 5	
SUITABLE FOR CHILDREN: 9	

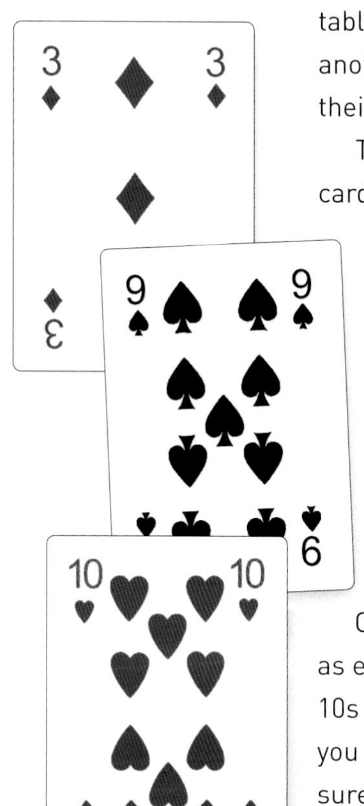

The dealer shuffles the deck and deals three cards to each player. Then places the rest of the pack in the middle of the table and turns over the top card, saying the value of the card out loud - kings, queens and jacks are 10, and the rest, apart from 3s, 9s and 10s, are at face value.

The next player puts a card on the discard pile, saying out loud the total value of the two cards, and so on around the table. And as each player puts a card down they must pick up another from the main pile. (If a player forgets to pick up after their discard, they must play on with only two cards.)

The object of the game is to avoid taking the total of the cards over 99, and this is where the 3s, 10s and 9s come in. If the player before you adds a card that makes the total 99, you can put down a 3 or a 9 to keep the total at 99, or a 10 to take it back to 89. A 3 means 99, a 9 means "stays the same" and a 10 means minus 10.

If a player cannot avoid going over 99, they lose a life. (And once a player has lost all three lives they are out of the game.) All the cards are put on the discard pile, and this is placed at the bottom of the pack, and the next hand is dealt.

On the whole it is as well to get rid of your high value cards as early in the game as possible and hold on to any 3s, 9s and 10s until you need them. However, if you have a strong hand, you can put down a 3 and call 99 as soon as you like, but make sure you are covered in case it comes round to you again!

Authors

PLAYERS: 2-9

DECK: FULL

SCORE SHEET: YES

SIMPLICITY FACTOR: 8

SKILL FACTOR: 5

SUITABLE FOR CHILDREN: 9

The aim of the game is to collect as many sets of four cards as you can.

All the cards are dealt out and the player to the left of the dealer begins by asking any of the other players for a particular card. The only rule is, that if he asks for a queen, he must already have one queen in his hand. If the player asked has the card, he must hand it over. And another card can be requested. If not, the player who was asked for a card, can ask for one in his turn. So the game continues in this way until all 13 sets have been collected.

Once a player has a set he must put them face down in front of him. Each set is worth one point. So the winner is the player with the most points at the end of an agreed number of games.

If a player completes a set and has no more cards in his hand he is out of that game, and the right to ask passes to the player who gave him his last card.

You can gather up sets most quickly if you keep a careful eye on what is happening. If you have a king and you notice that a player has just collected three kings... then you will know who to ask for kings when your turn comes!

Concentration

PLAYERS: ANY

DECK: FULL

SCORE SHEET: NO

SIMPLICITY FACTOR: 7

SKILL FACTOR: 8

SUITABLE FOR CHILDREN: 10

A long way from the likes of Stud Poker or Contract Bridge, this is a traditional parlor game that loses nothing by being played with playing cards instead of a "purpose built" concentration pack.

A whole pack (including jokers, if you like) is dealt out face-down on a table so they are not covering up or touching each other. (You'll need a pretty big table!) The first player turns over any one card so everybody can see it, then puts it back face-down in the same place and repeats the process with another. The other players, in turn, do the same. The aim is to pick pairs matched by value and color—the red jacks, the black fives and so on—which are then taken out of the game and placed in front of the player who picked them. This player then has another turn and continues until he fails to match two cards. Where the concentration comes in is in remembering cards' positions in order to make the matches. The winner is the player who finishes the game with the most pairs in front of them.

Did you know?

Also known as Memory, Pairs or Pelmanism this simple but surprisingly challenging matching game is an effective way to develop short-term memory. The name, Pelmanism, which can also mean a system of training to improve the memory, comes from the Pelman Institute for the Scientific Development of Mind Memory, founded in London in 1898.

Beggar My Neighbor

PLAYERS: TWO UPWARDS

SCORE SHEET: NO

DECK: FULL, USE TWO FOR SIX OR MORE PLAYERS

ACES: HIGH

ORIGIN: GREAT BRITAIN

SIMPLICITY FACTOR: 8

SKILL FACTOR: 0

SUITABLE FOR CHILDREN: 9

Though classically for two players only, there's no reason why Beggar My Neighbor can't involve as many as you like. All the cards are dealt out into face-down piles in front of each player. The first player turns up his top card into the middle of the table (the pot), the player on his left then does the same, and so on around the table until a player turns up a picture card or an ace.

The player to his left must now turn up "forfeit cards" on to the pot: one if the card turned up was a jack, two if it was a queen, three for a king, and four for an ace. If, during the forfeit, the player concerned turns up a picture card or an ace, the player to his left has to make the relevant forfeit.

Did you know?

Beggar My Neighbor, also known as Beat Jack Out of Doors and Strip Jack Naked, is a simple card game with similar principles to the card game War. Its exact origins are not known, but it was probably invented in Britain in the mid 19th century and has been a popular game there ever since, especially with children. It appears in Charles Dickens's novel *Great Expectations* (published in 1861), as the only card game that Pip, the hero of the story, knows how to play.

If the forfeit is paid entirely in spot cards, the player who turned up the card that forced the forfeit picks up the pot and puts it, face-down, under his own pile.

When a player has run out of cards, he drops out. The winner is the player who ends up with all the cards.

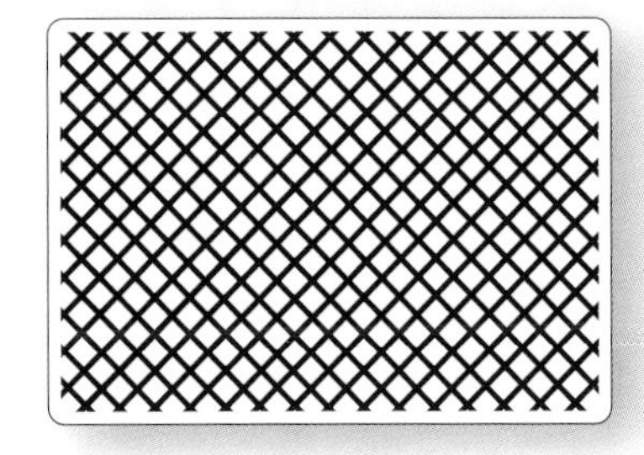

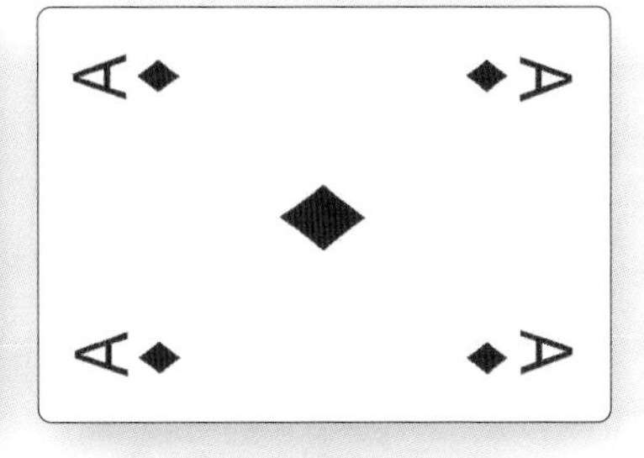

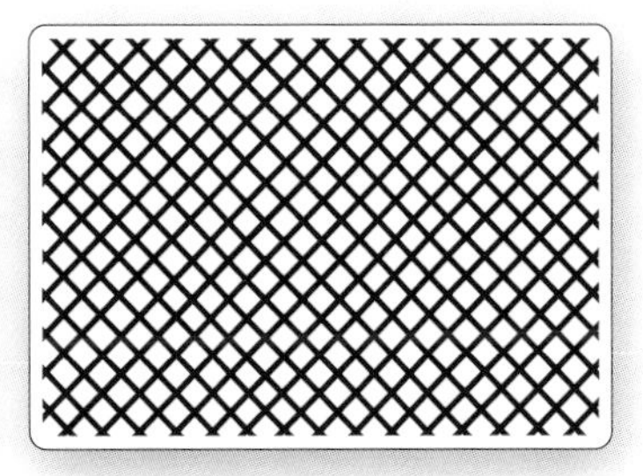

An ace forfeits four cards

Brag

PLAYERS: ANY
DECK: FULL
SCORE SHEET: NO
ACES: HIGH
ORIGIN: ENGLAND
SIMPLICITY FACTOR: 10
SKILL FACTOR: 3
SUITABLE FOR CHILDREN: 7
SUITABLE FOR GAMBLING: 8

The English forerunner of Poker, Brag never really made it in the U.S., where it is often seen as "Poker with the skill taken out". Each player is dealt three cards and hands are compared to see whose can be arranged into the most valuable combination (see scoring). The highest hand wins. In classic English Brag there are three wild cards, Braggarts, the jack of clubs, the nine of diamonds and the ace of diamonds.

SCORING

Three aces is the highest hand, progressing down to three twos. Running flushes (cards of the same suit in sequential

The three Braggarts

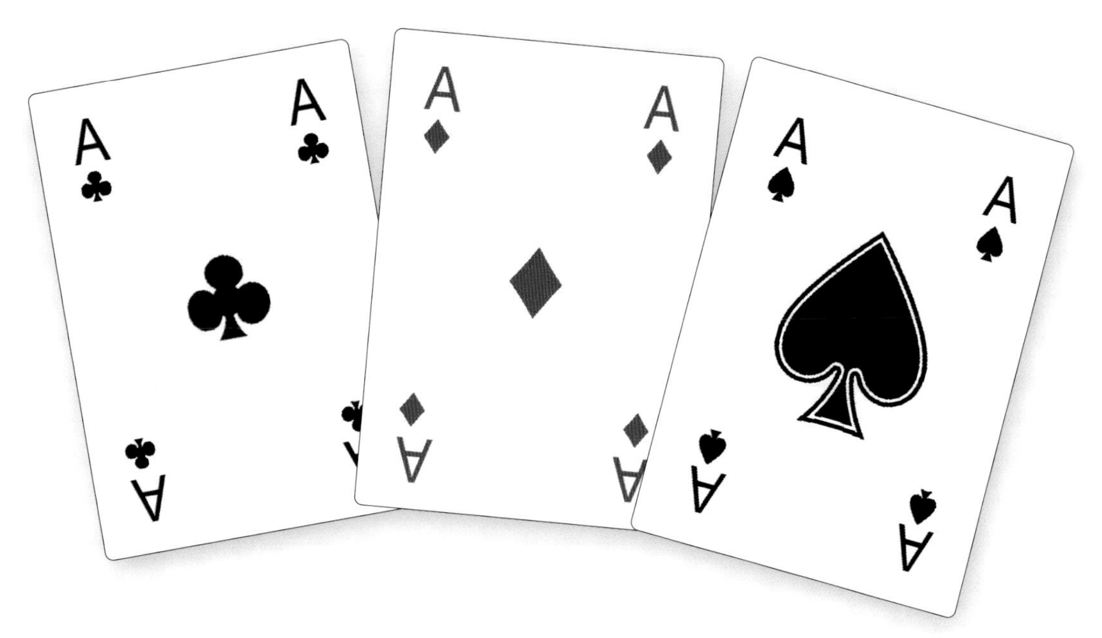

Brag's highest hand

order), flushes (cards of the same suit) and runs (cards in sequential order, not of the same suit) using all three cards, are below three of a kind in that order and are ranked according to the highest card in each hand. (Some rules don't include these three combinations, but there's nothing wrong with them being used, provided all players have agreed to it beforehand.)

Pairs are below anything that uses all three cards. If two pairs are numerically the same, the player with the highest denomination spare card wins. There is no hierarchy among the four suits. In every case, a "natural" hand beats a hand involving a braggart to achieve the same result.

If no player can make any combination, the hand containing the highest card is the winner.

BETTING

Betting goes round the table from the left of the dealer, with each player seeing, raising or dropping out (see Poker), until those remaining agree to compare hands for the pot, exactly as in poker.

Variations

AMERICAN BRAG

Involves eight Braggarts—all the jacks and all the nines—and all Braggarts are of equal value, but a hand with a Braggart in it outranks the same naturally achieved hand. Thus three jacks is the highest score, followed by three nines.

FIVE-CARD BRAG

Each player is dealt five cards, discarding two, face-down, to leave their best hand, before any betting or comparison starts.

Giveaway

PLAYERS: TWO TO SIX
DECK: FULL
SCORE SHEET: NO
ACES: LOW
ORIGIN: GREAT BRITAIN
SIMPLICITY FACTOR: 7
SKILL FACTOR: 8
SUITABLE FOR CHILDREN: 8
SUITABLE FOR GAMBLING: 0

This is a game that requires a degree of quick wit to make up for the luck involved in the fact that players cannot see their own cards until they play them.

Giveaway can be played with up to six players. All cards are dealt out into face-down piles in front of the players. It doesn't really matter if they have slightly unequal amounts. The first player turns over his top card and if it is any of the four aces he puts it in the middle of the table and turns over another, which, if it's the two of the same suit as the ace, he puts it on top of the ace. If his first card isn't an ace, it is placed face-up in front of him. The next player then turns up his top card. If it is the next card in the suit and sequence to that on the centre pile or the previous player's pile, he can add it to that pile and play again. If he can't add a card to any piles, he places the card in front of him and play continues round the table.

The idea is to make sequences on any upturned card on the table. If a player has turned up a nine of clubs and any other player has either the ten or the eight showing he can add his card to their pile. Any player who can follow a sequence carries on turning cards until they can't, when the card is put on their own face-up pile.

When a player has played through all of the cards in his hand he inverts his face-up pile and carries on playing. The winner is the first to get rid of all his cards on to either the centre piles or other players' piles.

Newmarket

PLAYERS: THREE TO EIGHT

DECK: FULL, PLUS A SPARE PACK

ACES: LOW

SIMPLICITY FACTOR: 4

SKILL FACTOR: 2

SUITABLE FOR CHILDREN: 8

SUITABLE FOR GAMBLING: 8

This is a simple and enjoyable family gambling game, sometimes known as Boodle or Stops.

To begin with, a layout is required. The Ace of spades, the King of hearts, the Queen of clubs and the Jack of diamonds are taken from the spare deck of cards and placed in a square in the middle of the table. All the players need a number of counters or small sweets, ten to fifteen or so should be enough.

The cards are ranked from Ace lowest to King highest. The deal passes to the left at the end of each game.

Before the deal, the dealer places two counters on each card in the layout. Each player places one counter on each card in the layout.

The cards are then dealt out one by one amongst the players, along with an extra hand which is put to one side and is not used during play. Each player picks up his cards, and sorts them in to suits.

The player to the dealer's left plays any card he chooses. He can play any suit, but must play the lowest card in that suit that he has. He announces the number and suit of the card as he places it in front of him. Then whoever has the next highest card in the suit, places that card in front of him and so on. Play continues following sequence and suit, until no more cards can be played (this might be because the card is in the extra hand or has been played earlier). When play stops, the player who played the stop card, plays the lowest card he has of any suit, and play continues.

During play, the player who puts down any of the cards that appear in the layout, wins all the counters on that card. Play ends, when one of the players has played all his cards, and each of the other players gives him one counter for every card they have left. If you run out of counters you're out of the game.

Any counters unclaimed on the layout are left where they are and are added to the winnings for the next game. If, at the end of play, there are counters left unclaimed, the dealer deals the entire deck again, face up, amongst the players and the player who is dealt a card that matches a card in the layout wins the counters.

CHAPTER 3

Patience Games

Known in the USA as solitaire, patience games involve one player pitting his or her wits against the luck of the draw. The aim is generally to form suit sequences from Ace to King. Patience has the reputation of a simple game of chance, but in fact, very few patience games require no skill at all. Many players enjoy the soothing quality of laying out the cards in a specific order, but there is undoubtedly a need for clear-thinking and concentration during play. Specially-made patience cards are helpful, because the games often require the cards to be set out in a complicated pattern or arrangement, known as tableau.

Klondike

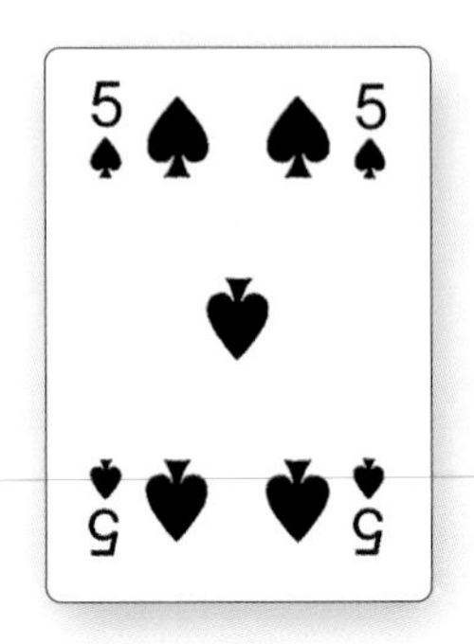

PLAYERS: ONE

DECK: FULL

SCORE SHEET: NO

ACES: LOW

ORIGIN: USA

SIMPLICITY FACTOR: 8

SKILL FACTOR: 7

SUITABLE FOR CHILDREN: 3

The most popular form of patience in the world, for many people in Europe and the U.S. Klondike is known as Patience or Solitaire, rather than by its true name.

A full deck is shuffled and seven cards are dealt in a row, with the first card (the one on the left) turned face-up. On top of these cards a second row of six is dealt, commencing with the first face-down card (second left) upon which a face-up card is dealt while the remaining five cards are covered with face-down cards. The next row is of five cards, following the same pattern. This continues until there is a triangular layout with the first column on the left being a face-up card and the last one on the right being six face-down cards with a face-up one at the bottom. The remaining cards are held in a face-down stack.

The object is to build up the suits in numerical order, starting from their respective aces. When the aces are face-up, uncovered or revealed through the deal of the deck, they are placed separately on the table. The twos of the same suit can then be placed on top of the aces and so on, so that four piles of cards, each a separate suit, are gradually built up.

In order to free up the face-down cards, the player builds descending numerical sequences of alternate red and black cards. As face-up cards are moved to put into a sequence or one of the suits being built, so the face-down card underneath it is turned over. Complete sequences can be moved to free up

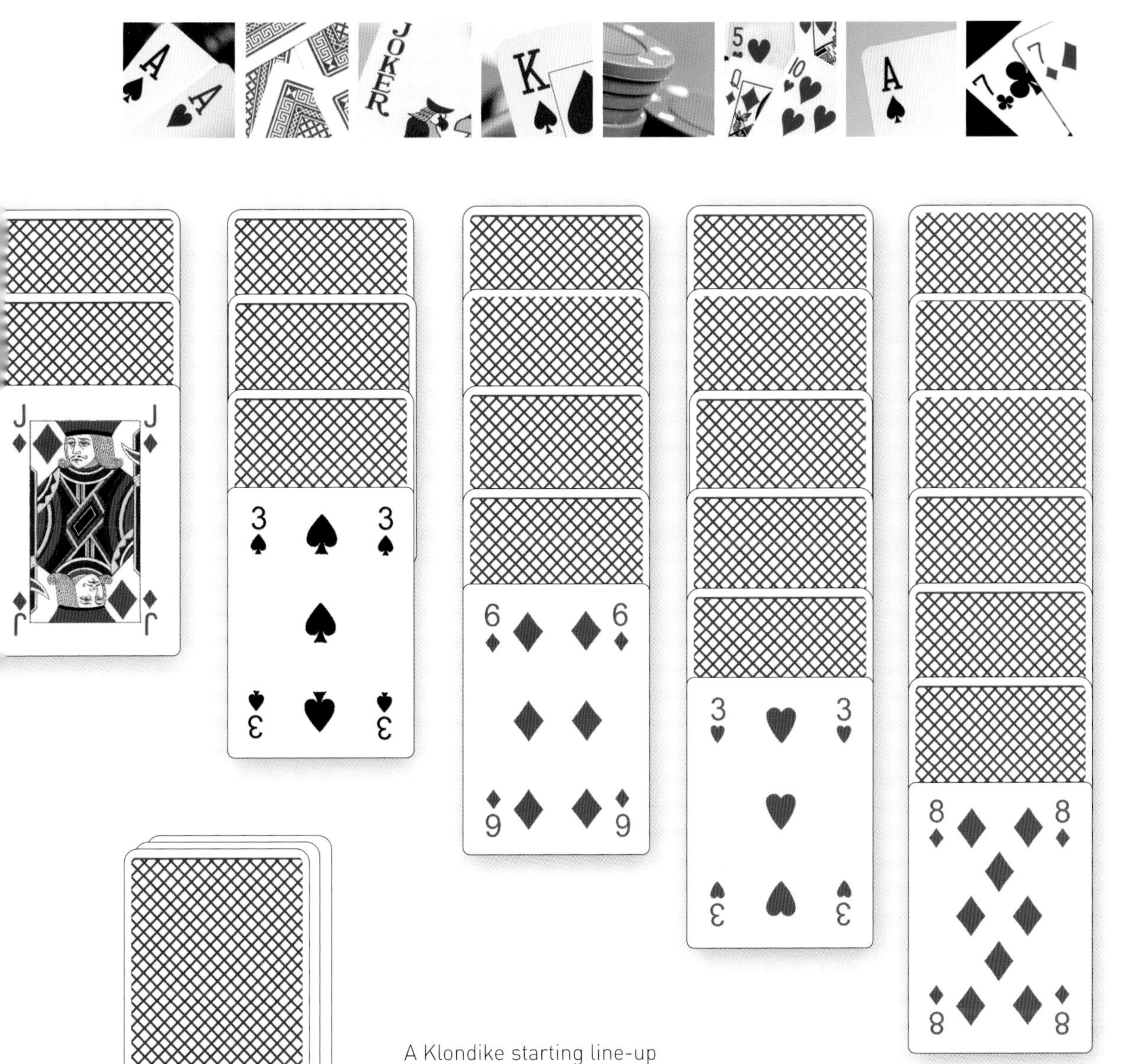

A Klondike starting line-up

the face-down card beneath them, but only kings or sequences starting with a king can be moved into an empty column.

When no movement is possible, every third card in the stack is turned up and any of these can be put into play. If this still yields no movement, then the dealt-out stack is turned face-down, the top card put on the bottom and it is dealt out again in parcels of three. If three consecutive deals produce no movement, the game is lost. To win, every suit must be collected, in ascending sequence, on top of its respective ace.

Labyrinth

PLAYERS: ONE

DECK: FULL

SIMPLICITY FACTOR: 4

SKILL FACTOR: 2

SUITABLE FOR CHILDREN: 3

This one-deck game of patience is simpler to set out than its name implies, but it will probably take quite a few attempts to play all the cards out.

To begin with, take the four aces from the deck and place them in a row. Then shuffle the rest of the deck, and deal, face up and from left to right, a row of eight cards.

The object is to build on the aces in ascending order and following suit. So any cards from the first row can be built on the aces. And new cards are dealt, from left to right, to fill these spaces. When all possible cards have been played, and any spaces filled, deal another row of eight and play as before.

Spaces can be filled in the first row, but spaces in subsequent rows must be left blank.

Carry on playing and dealing in the same way until there are no cards left in the deck.

Playable cards are the cards in the top and bottom rows. If a card is played from the top row, you can then play the card in the row below it, and then the one below that. Similarly, if you play a card from the bottom row, you can then play the card in the row above that, and so on. Only if the game gets "blocked" can you take any card from any of the rows.

Aces Up

PLAYERS: ONE

DECK: FULL

SCORE SHEET: NO

ACES: HIGH

ORIGIN: USA

SIMPLICITY FACTOR: 10

SKILL FACTOR: 2

SUITABLE FOR CHILDREN: 8

This game is also known as Idiot's Delight, but the name is a trifle unfair on a form of patience that is a fast-moving and fun, if unchallenging, distraction.

Four cards are dealt face-up next to each other and if a suit is represented more than once, the lower denomination card or cards are removed and placed on a discard pile. Four more cards are dealt on top of the others and into any spaces left by removed cards and the process is repeated. The game progresses as the removal of cards exposes cards that precipitate the removal of others. The next layer will only be dealt when there can be no further removal activity. Cards can be moved into empty spaces from the top of other piles. The player will have won if he is left with four aces on the table and all other cards on the discard pile. He will have been beaten if there are any other cards left in the piles once the last set of four has been dealt.

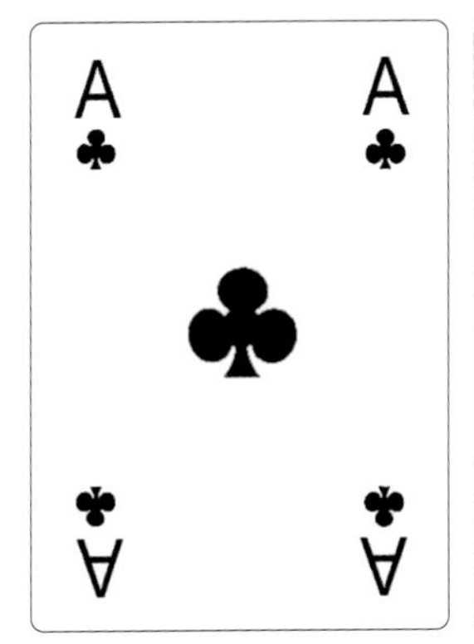

Clock Patience

PLAYERS: ONE
DECK: FULL
SCORE SHEET: NO
ACES: LOW
SIMPLICITY FACTOR: 10
SKILL FACTOR: 0
SUITABLE FOR CHILDREN: 8

A simple, fast-moving and entertaining form of patience, ideal for children as there's about a fifty per cent chance of winning. Thirteen face-down stacks of four cards are dealt out with twelve arranged in a circle like the numbers on a clock and the remaining stack put to one side of the "face". Of this stack, the top card is turned up and placed on the stack in the position of its number on the clock face. For example, a six would be put at the bottom of the circle, where the six is on a clock. The ace represents one o'clock, the jack eleven o'clock and the queen is midday.

When a card is placed on a stack, the bottom card from that stack is taken out, turned over and then put in its correct place from where the bottom card is taken and moved on to its correct place, and so on. If a king is turned up it will be put into a row in the centre of the "clock" and the next card will be taken from the pile that has been put aside. The idea is to turn all the cards in the clock face over before the fourth king is turned up and there are no more reserve cards to draw upon.

King Albert

PLAYERS: ONE

DECK: FULL

ACES: LOW

ORIGIN: USA

SIMPLICITY FACTOR: 7

SKILL FACTOR: 8

SUITABLE FOR CHILDREN: 7

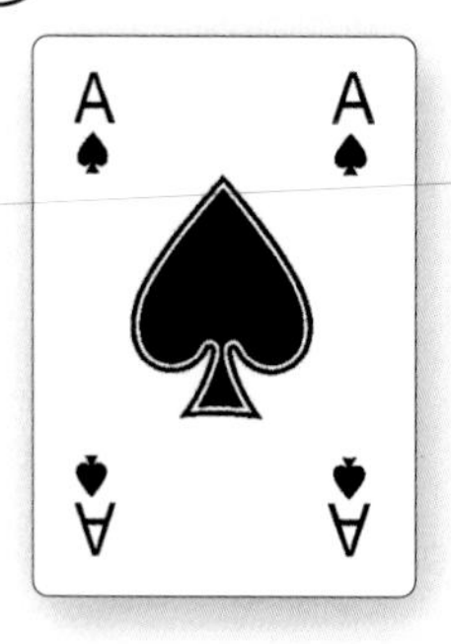

A variation of Klondike that requires slightly more skill and so is slightly more difficult to win.

All the cards are dealt out face-up in nine columns, with the one on the left having one card, and the far right one having nine. The seven cards left over are dealt into one face-up row at the foot of the layout.

The object is to build up the suits on the aces, once they are freed, but cards can only be moved singly, never as whole, pre-built sequences. However, unlike in Klondike, any card can be put into an empty column, thus with two empty columns sequences can be moved by "bouncing" alternate cards between the two columns. Cards are put into play from the face-up row only when no movement is possible on the layout. If all these reserve cards have been used and play is blocked before the four suits have been collected on the aces, the game is lost. If the suits have been collected it is won.

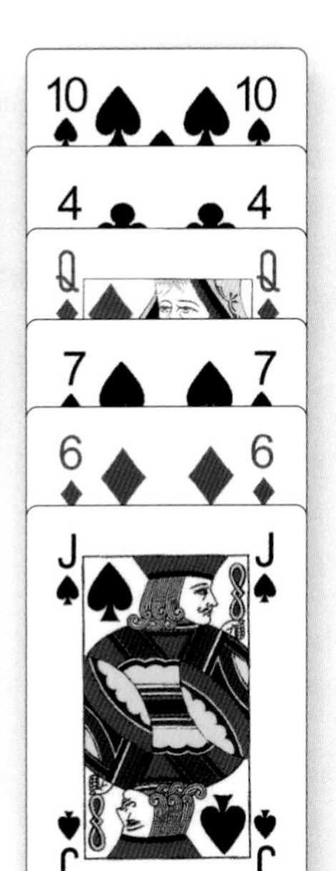

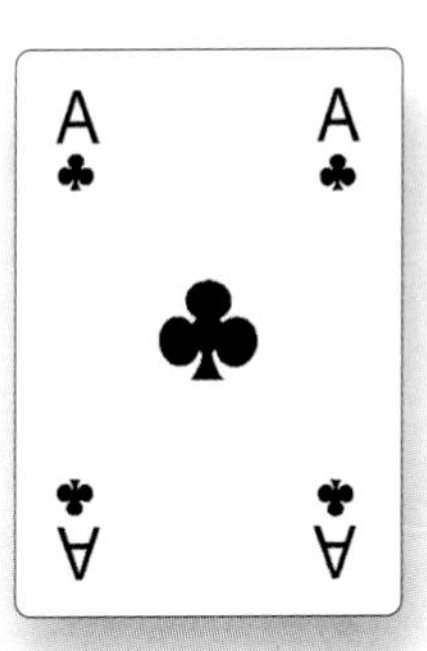

Monte Carlo

PLAYERS: ONE

DECK: FULL

SCORE SHEET: NO

ACES: HIGH

SIMPLICITY FACTOR: 9

SKILL FACTOR: 3

SUITABLE FOR CHILDREN: 10

A quick and easy game of patience that relies greatly on how the cards are dealt.

A full deck is shuffled and 20 cards are dealt face-up in four rows of five, with the remainder held as a pot. If any cards are adjacent to one of similar face value, horizontally, vertically or diagonally, the pair is removed and put in a pile. (If three cards of the same value are next to each other, only two can be removed at one time.) Once all pairs from the layout have been removed, cards are dealt from the stack to replenish the layout by filling the holes.

The object is to pair up all the cards and if the layout becomes such that no more pairing is possible, the game is lost.

Did you know?

Patience games are also known as Solitaire. Solitaire comes from an old French word which pretty much means patience.

All Patience games are devised for one player and have varying degrees of complication in layout and play. Most are based on the principle of playing out a deck of cards by building in number and suit order on foundations, usually aces.

There are many different patience games and Lady Adelaide Cadogan is thought to have published the first book of Patience games in English in 1870. It was called *The Illustrated Games of Patience.*

Famous world leaders who are said to have enjoyed a game of Patience include Franklin D Roosevelt (his favorite game was Spider) and Napoleon.

Royal Marriage

PLAYERS: ONE

DECK: FULL

SCORE SHEET: NO

ORIGIN: ENGLAND

SIMPLICITY FACTOR: 9

SKILL FACTOR: 3

SUITABLE FOR CHILDREN: 8

Often called Betrothal, the aim of this romantically inclined patience game is to unite a king and queen that have been set apart from each other.

To start, a king and queen of the same suit are removed from a full deck while it is being shuffled and cut, and are placed one each on the top and bottom of the deck, (it doesn't matter which of the cards goes where). The cards are dealt out across the table in a face-up line. Every time a card appears with cards of the same suit as each other on either side—for example, ten of hearts, four of clubs, three of hearts—the card in the middle (in this case the four of clubs) is removed. The gap closed up and the deal continues.

The object is to remove all the cards so that the selected royal couple end up next to each other on the table. If all the cards are dealt out and it is not possible to remove any, the game is lost.

A royal marriage

Trefoil

PLAYERS: ONE

DECK: FULL

ACES: LOW

ORIGIN: FRANCE

SIMPLICITY FACTOR: 8

SKILL FACTOR: 3

SUITABLE FOR CHILDREN: 6

A deceptively tricky game of patience that, on first approach, appears very easy but is really rather difficult to win.

All four aces are removed from a full deck, and placed face-up on the table as bases for building up their respective suits. The remainder of the cards are then shuffled and dealt into sixteen face-up piles of three, which are fanned out to resemble the "trefoils" or three-leafed clovers of the title. The idea is to build up the suits from two upward with top cards from any of the trefoils. However, to free up cards locked inside trefoils, top cards can be moved on to other trefoil top cards—provided they are of the same suit and numerically descending—to create descending builds. Whole builds can also be transferred in this way.

If all moves are "blocked"—no cards can be placed on descending builds or the suits—trefoils without builds on them are gathered up, shuffled and re-dealt, once again as threes, with any left over making the final trefoil of one or two cards. Three such re-deals are allowed, and if a game gets blocked after that, it is lost.

Variations

MIDNIGHT OIL

Here the aces are dealt out as part of the trefoils and have to be freed up like any other card in order to serve as bases.

HOUSE IN THE WOODS

Midnight Oil played with two decks shuffled together and the eight aces dealt into the trefoils.

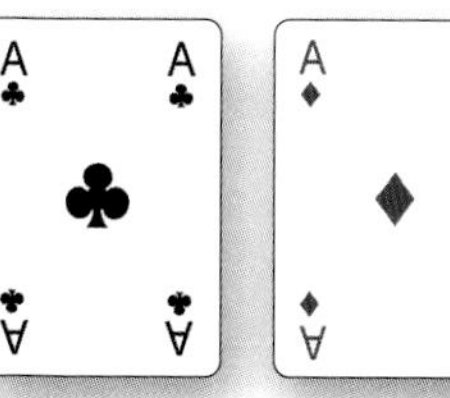

CHAPTER 4

Hearts Games

This family of games are straightforward and fun with a touch of spice. Variations have developed and there is usually a big discussion before play begins, because everyone has their favorite. The object is to avoid winning tricks and clocking up points, and often it is best to aim not to win any tricks at all because penalty points are incurred for certain cards, usually hearts and the Queen of Spades. However, some games have developed a twist where it can pay to go for the lot, and thereby reduce your score. In Jacks and Polignac the Jacks are the cards to avoid.

Hearts

PLAYERS: THREE TO EIGHT

DECK: FULL

SCORE SHEET: NO

ACES: HIGH

ORIGIN: FRANCE

SIMPLICITY FACTOR: 8

SKILL FACTOR: 8

SUITABLE FOR CHILDREN: 7

SUITABLE FOR GAMBLING: 7

A straightforward, enjoyable game that has been spiced up over the centuries with a number of different variations, Hearts can be played with between three and eight players.

In its simplest form, all the cards are dealt out face-down—to keep the hands equal up to four low denomination cards (other than hearts) will be removed—and each player looks at his hand. There are no trumps, so tricks are won by the highest card of the lead suit, and only players unable to follow suit can discard. Tricks are amassed in front of the players who won them and the winner leads the next trick. When all are played, the cards are turned face-up and each player scores one point for every heart card in his haul.

Scores are totalled, hand by hand, and games finish as soon as a player has 50 points, with the winner being the one with the lowest total. The idea is therefore not to take tricks with hearts in them.

If agreed in advance, after looking at his hand each player can pass four cards to the player on his left.

Don't take tricks with hearts in them

BETTING

On a hand-by-hand basis, every player puts in a prescribed amount for each heart he's left holding and the winner takes the pot. If being scored cumulatively, an average of the players' totals is taken and those above it put the amount they are over it in the pot while those below it take out the amount they are below it.

Variations

BLACK MARIA

The most common variation, in which the player who ends up with the queen of spades scores an extra 13 points, but the player finishing up with the jack of diamonds deducts 10 points from his score.

BLACK WIDOW

The same as Black Maria, except that the full 52 cards are used regardless of how many players. Any cards left over after the deal—the widows—are given to the winner of the first trick, who is the only player permitted to look at them, to be counted in his score for that hand.

The Black Maria

PINK LADY

As Black Maria, but with the queen of hearts also counting for 13 points.

TAKE ALL HEARTS

In this version, if any player, in any of the above variations, takes all the hearts and any other penalty or bonus cards, points are deducted instead of added to his total.

Jacks

PLAYERS: THREE

DECK: FULL

SCORE SHEET: NO

ACES: HIGH

ORIGIN: FRANCE

SIMPLICITY FACTOR: 9

SKILL FACTOR: 7

SUITABLE FOR CHILDREN: 7

SUITABLE FOR GAMBLING: 5

Sometimes called Knaves, this game is not dissimilar to Whist but it is played with just three players and has a different cumulative scoring system.

The whole of a full deck is dealt out to the three players, with the remaining card turned over to establish trumps. The thirteen tricks are competed for as in Whist—the highest in the led suit or a trump wins—and players collect the tricks they've won in front of them. Once a hand is complete, players count their scores as one point for each trick won, but tricks containing each of the four jacks incur penalty points so hands can end up with minus scores. The idea is therefore to take as many tricks as possible, but to avoid the ones with jacks in them. Games are usually stopped when a player has reached 20 points.

SCORING

One point is gained for each trick won, but the following points are deducted from players' totals if they finish up with tricks with jacks in them: jack of spades—one point; jack of clubs—two; jack of diamonds—three; jack of hearts—four.

BETTING

Having prearranged a cash-for-points value, the two losing players would pay the winner whatever the difference was between their hand and the winning total.

Avoid the jacks

Variations

POLIGNAC

The classic French form of Jacks, dating back to the 17th century, and played by between four and six players. For four players cards between two and five are removed, for five or six players the black sevens are taken out too. The idea is to score as few points as possible, no points are awarded for tricks, one is given for tricks containing the jacks of hearts, diamonds and clubs, while the jack of spades—the "polignac"—counts for two. If a player declares himself a "general" at the start of a hand, it means he intends to take all the tricks. If he does he deducts five points from his score, if not everybody else does and the jacks score as usual. Games finish after a prearranged number of hands and the scores are tallied.

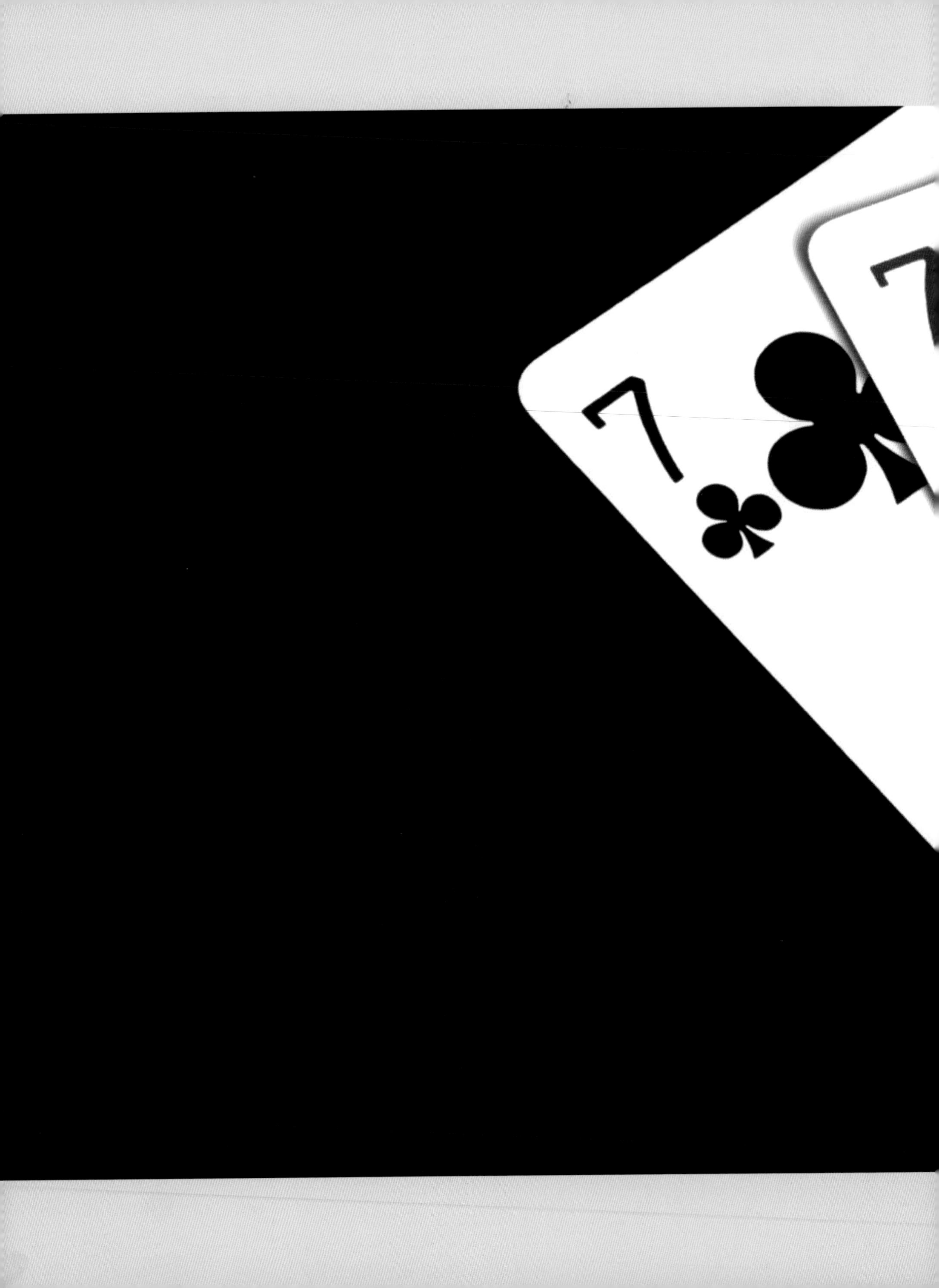

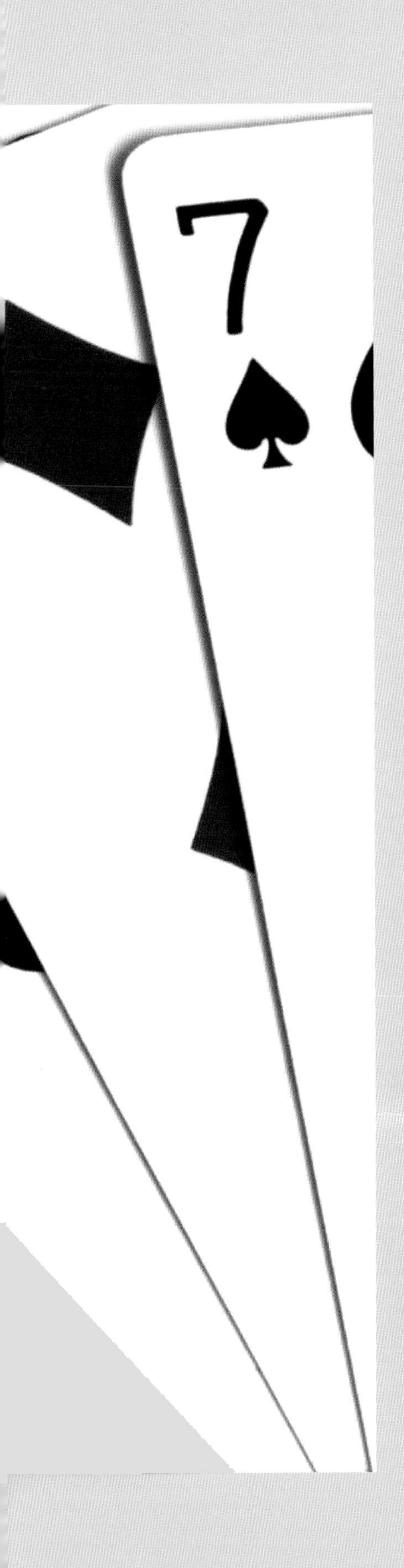

CHAPTER 5

Games for Two

If you're looking for a game for two players, this is the section for you. Bezique is a French game with a unique and complicated scoring system, and some interesting variations. Piquet is around 500 years old, and although it has been updated over the years, it still reflects the courtly manners of a 15th-century palace. Klaberjass is a complex and fascinating game, sometimes known as Klob or Klobby, and is probably one of the most widely played games for two people. On a lighter note, Jiggery-pokery is a brilliant game of bluff and chance, and Pisha Pasha is a variation of that old favorite Snap!—a fun, simple game for young children.

Bezique

PLAYERS: TWO

DECK: DOUBLE PIQUET PACK

SCORE SHEET: YES

ACES: LOW

ORIGIN: FRANCE

SIMPLICITY FACTOR: 1

SKILL FACTOR: 9

SUITABLE FOR CHILDREN: 2

SUITABLE FOR GAMBLING: 6

The original 16th-century French version of what became Pinochle, Bezique is played by two players, with 64 cards. The game is in two parts and has a unique and rather complicated scoring system.

Two piquet decks (a piquet deck has a high ace and no cards below the seven) are shuffled together and eight cards dealt to each player—in the game's classical form these would be dealt as two threes then a two. The top card of the remainder determines trumps and is put on the bottom of the pile. If the non-dealer holds the seven in the trump suit, he can exchange it for the up card, and gains ten points. Whoever holds the other seven of trumps gains ten points when he plays it. The player other than the dealer leads. The dealer does not have to follow suit, but the only way to win the trick is either by playing a higher card of the suit that led or by trumping. If both players play the same card, the player that went first wins the trick.

The player who wins the trick adds it to his hand. He can then make melds (groups of cards of the same numerical value or same suit or in numerical sequence) with his hands and lay them down face-up on the table. One meld may be "declared" and the score it earns added to that player's total. The trick's winner then takes the top card from the remaining deck, the trick's loser takes the next card. The trick's winner then replenishes his hand to bring the number of cards held back to eight.

The game continues with cards that have been laid down in melds remaining available for play. Cards may be re-used in

subsequent declarations providing they are not the same type of meld as the card was originally used in. A jack of clubs that has already featured in a four-jack declaration can be re-declared in a king, queen, jack meld, but not another combination of four jacks. Once the deck has been exhausted, play goes on with opponents having to follow the lead suit if they can, until all tricks are played out.

Games can last for just that hand, or until one player amasses a prescribed number of points.

Bezique

SCORING

Melds are worth:

- Double bezique—500
- Trump sequence—
  A, 10, J, Q, K of trumps—250
- Any four aces—100
- Any four kings—80
- Any four queens—60
- Any four jacks—40
- Royal marriage (king and
  queen of trumps)—40
- Bezique (queen and jack of any suit)—40
- Plain marriage—king and queen of any suit other than trumps—20
- Dix—when the up-card is exchanged for the seven of trumps—10 (each).

AT THE END

- The winner of the final trick scores 10 points.
- Every "brisque"—an ace or a 10 contained in a meld—scores the holder 10 points each.

PENALTIES

- If a player draws out of turn his opponent scores 10.
- If a player's hand contains more than eight cards his opponent scores 100.

A trump sequence

BETTING

If playing one hand at a time, the difference in the two scores is translated into a pre-arranged fiscal value. If playing up to a points limit, the amount of the loser's shortfall would be converted into cash.

Variations

THREE-HANDED BEZIQUE

The same as above, but played with three piquet decks (96 cards) and three players.

RUBICON BEZIQUE

Played with four decks (128 cards) by two people who are dealt nine cards each. The first marriage declared determines trumps, games are one hand long and the scoring involves the following extra situations:

- Quadruple bezique—4500
- Triple bezique—1500
- A sequence (ace, 10, jack, queen, king) other than trumps—150
- Carte Blanche—being dealt a first hand that contains no picture cards—50
- Taking the final trick—50 points
- Winning the game –500.

Total scores are counted in 100s, being rounded down, so 1260 would become 1200. However, if the difference between winning and losing is less than 100 points, the winner will have won by 100. Brisques are only counted if the scores are tied, or added in if the loser is "rubiconed", i.e. his total score is less than 1000. If this is the case, his score is added to the winner's, as is 320 for all the brisques that the winner holds and the win bonus is doubled to 1000. (In all variations of Bezique, it is only the loser that is rubiconed, even if both players fail to reach the prescribed score.)

SIX-DECK BEZIQUE

Sometimes called Chinese Bezique, this is played with six piquet decks (192 cards). Games are decided after one deal, players start with 12 cards, brisques never count and the following scores are added to Rubicon Bezique's system:

- Four trump aces—1000
- Four trump kings—800
- Four trump queens—600
- Four trump jacks—400
- Four trump tens—900
- Carte Blanche—250
- Taking the last trick—250
- Winning the game—1000
- The loser is rubiconed for a score of less than 3000.

EIGHT-DECK BEZIQUE

Eight piquet decks (256 cards) are used and the players are dealt 15 cards each. The rules are the same as for Six-Deck Bezique with these additions to the score board:

- Quintuple Bezique —9000
- Five trump aces—2000
- Five trump kings—1600
- Five trump queens—1200
- Five trump jacks—800
- Five trump tens—1800
- The loser is rubiconed for a score of less than 5000.

Pisha Pasha

PLAYERS: TWO
DECK: FULL
SCORE SHEET: NO
ACES: HIGH
ORIGIN: EASTERN EUROPE
SIMPLICITY FACTOR: 10
SUITABLE FOR CHILDREN: 10

One step up from Snap! this quick, easy and fun two-handed game is for very young children.

A full deck of cards is dealt into two face-down piles, with one being placed in front of each player. The players simultaneously turn cards over to form separate face-up piles in front of each of them. When both players turn up cards of the same suit, they call "Pisha Pasha" and whoever has played the card of the higher numerical value takes both upturned piles and puts them on the bottom of their face-down stash. The winner is the first player to capture all the cards, but if their stash runs out while the other player still has cards, the face-up pile will be turned over and used to continue the game.

Pisha Pasha

Klaberjass

PLAYERS: TWO

SCORE SHEET: YES

DECK: NO CARDS LOWER THAN SEVEN

ACES: HIGH

ORIGIN: EASTERN EUROPE

SIMPLICITY FACTOR: 4

SKILL FACTOR: 9

SUITABLE FOR CHILDREN: 3

SUITABLE FOR GAMBLING: 6

An involved but fascinating game of Eastern European origin that became very popular in the U.S. Sometimes this game is called Klob or Klobber.

Klaberjass is played by two players with a piquet deck (no cards lower than a seven). The aim is to take tricks and make melds. The cards' rankings are rearranged thus: in the non-trumps suits the 10 is moved to rank in between the ace and the king as the second highest valued card, as it is in the trumps suit, but with the jack and the nine, in that order, ranking above the ace. This means that the non-trumps suit runs A, 10, K, Q, J, 9, 8, 7 and the trumps suit runs J, 9, A, 10, K, Q, 8, 7.

Six cards are dealt to each player—this can be done as two parcels of three. The next card is turned up to signify trumps, which the players then have the choice to accept or reject. The non-dealer goes first and can declare "Accept" meaning he takes the suit as trumps, "Pass" meaning the bid passes to the dealer, or "Schmeiss" meaning he would prefer that this hand was folded and the cards re-dealt. The dealer then has the chance to make the same bids. If both players pass, the bidding comes round to the non-dealer again who has the chance to "make" trumps by naming any suit he wants. If he passes for a second time, the dealer has the chance to make trumps. If he, too, passes again, the hands are folded and the cards re-dealt. If both declare "Schmeiss" then the hands are folded. If trumps have been accepted rather than made, a player who has the seven of that suit (the "dix") may exchange it for the card that is turned up to signify trumps.

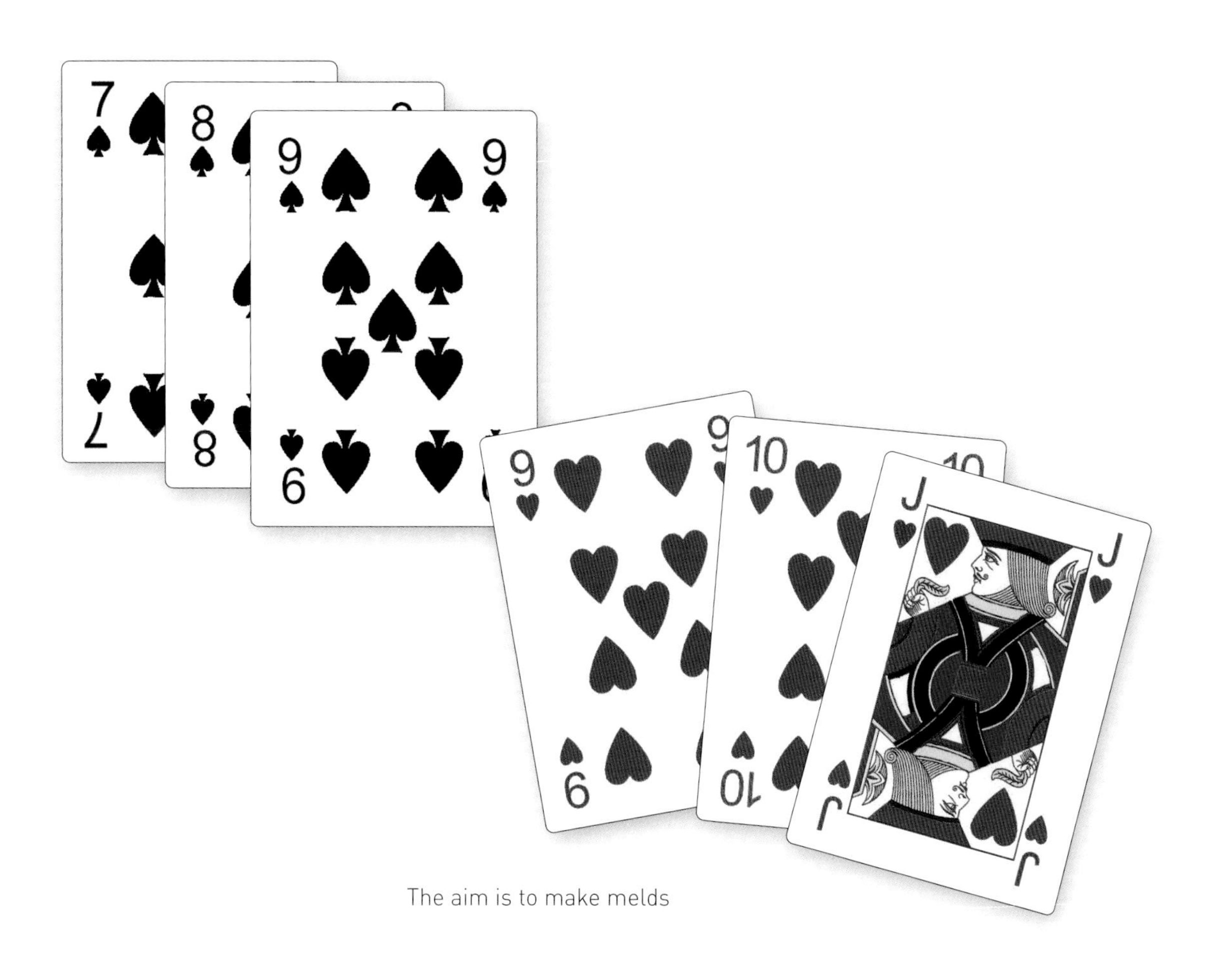

The aim is to make melds

Both players will now proceed to make melds of running flushes within their hands. The non-dealer declares his highest value meld and the dealer attempts to match it. This is done in remarkably formal language. The non-dealer announces a meld by saying "meld of 20 (or 50)". The dealer replies "Good", which means he can't match it and concedes; "Not good" which means he can beat it or "How high?" meaning he has the same and the players must compare top cards. In the event of a tied top card, if one suit is trumps it wins. If neither is then neither player scores. Whoever wins the declaration shows his opponent his winning meld and can score for any other he shows, the loser scores no points at all.

The idea, once play begins, is to win tricks with certain cards in them and score a prescribed schedule of points that are added to meld scores.

When the scores are counted up for each hand, if the player who accepted or made trumps scores less than his opponent, his score is given to his opponent and the first player scores nothing for the hand. If the player who didn't chose trumps scores lower, he keeps his score.

SCORING

Scores are as follows:

- Three-card meld—20
- Four-card meld—50
- Jack of trumps ("jass")—20
- Nine of trumps ("menel")—14
- Any ace—11
- Any ten—10
- Any king—4
- Any queen—3
- Any jack other than of trumps—2
- For taking the last trick—10
- King and queen of trumps (a "bella")—20 bonus points (this can be made by either player if they hold and declare a "bella").

Jiggery-pokery

PLAYERS: TWO

DECK: 3 COMPLETE SUITS–SPADES, CLUBS AND DIAMONDS

SCORE SHEET: YES

ACES: LOW

SIMPLICITY FACTOR: 8

SKILL FACTOR: 6

SUITABLE FOR CHILDREN: 7

This is a simple game of bluff and chance, with plenty of opportunities for misleading your opponent, hence the name!

One player takes all the clubs and the other takes the spades. The diamonds are shuffled, and put in the middle of the table, face down.

The aim is to win the highest value of diamonds—the King is worth 13, the Queen 12 and the Jack 11. The Ace is worth 1 and the rest are face value.

To start, the top diamond face is turned face up. Each player then places a card on the table, which is their bid for the diamond. When both players are ready, the cards are turned over, and the highest card (Ace low, King high) wins the diamond. The diamond is taken by the winner and put to one side. And the two black cards are put in a discard pile. Then the next diamond is turned over, and play continues in this way.

If the players bet cards of the same value, the two bid cards are discarded and the diamond is placed beside the pile for the next round. The next diamond is turned up, the players bid, and the winner takes both diamonds.

Pinochle

PLAYERS: TWO

SCORE SHEET: YES

DECK: TWO DECKS WITH EVERYTHING BELOW NINES REMOVED

ACES: HIGH

ORIGIN: ITALY

SIMPLICITY FACTOR: 3

SKILL FACTOR: 8

SUITABLE FOR CHILDREN: 2

SUITABLE FOR GAMBLING: 8

Of Italian origin, Pinochle remains one of the most popular two-handed card games in the U.S. Although it appears complicated, it is a game that seldom fails to repay the effort put into learning it. Scores are tallied for melds made and tricks taken that include certain scoring cards.

The game is played with two decks that have had everything lower than the nines removed, leaving 48 cards. The values are rearranged so that the ten ranks in between the ace and the king as the second highest card in each suit.

Each player is dealt 12 cards in lots of three, and the next card is turned up to signify trumps. The players then play out a trick, which will be won in the usual manner, and the player who won it can put down a meld in front of him. Only one meld is played per turn, and cards used in melds can be used in future melds or played in tricks.

Before the next trick is played, each player will take up a card from the stockpile, and the game continues with each player having 12 cards in his hand (including the meld) until the stockpile is exhausted. After the stockpile is used up, no more melds will be made and the melds in front of each player are taken back into their hand. The last twelve tricks are then played out in the usual way.

Once all the tricks have been played, the tricks are turned face-up and scored for the honor cards contained in them. The winner of the last trick also scores ten bonus points.

The winner of a game of pinochle is the first player to 1000.

SCORING

The melds are scored as follows:

- A, 10, K, Q, J of trumps—150
- King and queen of trumps (a "royal marriage")—40
- King and queen of any other suit (a "plain marriage")—20
- Queen of spades and jack of diamonds ("pinochle")—40
- Four aces (must all be of different suits)—100
- Four kings (must all be of different suits)—80
- Four queens (must all be of different suits)—60
- Four jacks (must all be of different suits)—40.

If the card turned over for trumps is a nine (the "dix") the dealer scores 10 points. If the dix was not revealed as the upturned card and a player has picked it up during the game, he can declare it and receive 10 bonus points.

In the tricks, aces score 11 points; tens score 10; kings—4; queens—3 and jacks—2. Each trick score is rounded up to the next unit of 10 if it ends in a 7, an 8 or a 9; and it is rounded down to the previous 10 if it is below 7.

Pinochle—ten points

Piquet

PLAYERS: TWO

SCORE SHEET: YES

DECK: NOTHING LOWER THAN A SEVEN

ACES: HIGH

ORIGIN: FRANCE OR ENGLAND

SIMPLICITY FACTOR: 2

SKILL FACTOR: 8

SUITABLE FOR CHILDREN: 3

SUITABLE FOR GAMBLING: 7

Although much reduced in popularity these days, Piquet continues to enjoy a small but enthusiastic following. It is seen by many card players as one of the best games for two players. It may seem complicated at first, but it is in fact a logical and simple game that is well worth mastering.

Played by two players, it is this game's use of the abbreviated 32-card deck (nothing lower than a seven) that gave rise to the term "piquet pack". Each player is dealt twelve cards in six lots of two and the remaining eight cards are placed face-down in one pile of three and one of five. Now the game (called a "partie") can begin and the idea is to win points by making melds and winning tricks. The process by which this is done is in four discernible stages.

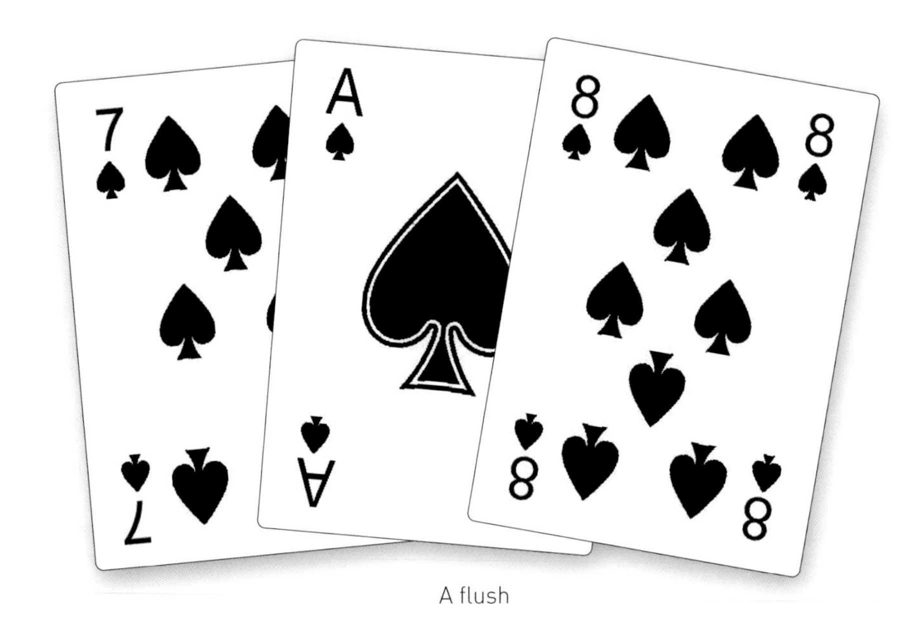

A flush

1) The Discard

The dealer discards up to five cards, replacing them from the stockpile of five, and then looks at any of the five he decides not to take up, without showing them to his opponent. The non-dealer then discards up to any of the number left in both stockpiles combined, and look at any of the cards he doesn't take up.

2) Making Combinations

The players arrange their hands into combinations of flushes, numerically sequential flushes and numerical groupings, which will be matched against the opponent's respective groupings. Cards from their hands can be used in more than one combination. At this point, they will decide which of their combinations they will "declare", which means to match against their opponent's.

3) Declaring Combinations

In classic piquet this is done with a formality that verges on the tedious, and although the process is explained below, it is rarely adhered to:

The non-dealer will first announce his longest flush (or "point") by saying "A point of ..." If the dealer can't match it he replies "Good" and concedes the points. If he can beat it he replies "Not good" and takes the points himself. If he can match it he asks "How many?" and the non-dealer replies "A point of ..., I score ..." and states the numerical value of his point. The dealer responds either with "Good" meaning he can't beat it, "Not good" meaning he can or "Equal" if his is the same value. If this happens the points are abandoned.

At the end of each point declaration, the winner has to declare his winning point and the score he got for it: "A point of ..., I score ..."

Next the non-dealer will declare his longest running flush, or "sequence" as it is called. To declare a sequence, the conversation is essentially the same except the announcement made would be "A sequence of ..." In the event of a tie the dealer will say "How high?", which precipitates the announcement of the highest card.

Finally the non-dealer declares his best meld, with the declaration "A trio of ..." or "A quatorze of ..." Of course, melds cannot tie.

4) The Play

After the declarations have finished, the tricks are played for in the usual manner but without a trump suit.

Scores are totalled after each hand, and the winner is the player with the highest number of points after the prescribed number of hands, or the first to reach "rubicon" or 100 points.

SCORING

It is possible for either player to score 10 points in between the deal and the discard if they announce a "carte blanche"—a hand featuring no court cards.

When the two players match their best "points", the one with the longest will score one point for each card in it. If two "points" contain the same number of cards, the numerical value is totalled, with court cards counting as 10, aces as 11 and the point with the highest value wins. Again, one point is awarded for each card. Players can only score for the one flush they decide to declare, even if they have others in their hand.

A short history of Piquet

Pronounced "pee-kay" or "picket". Piquet is a 500-year-old card game with some interesting and unusual features that put it in a class of its own.

The name may come from the French word *piquer* which means to prick or sting. Although, some say that the name simply comes from that of its inventor, who thought up the game to amuse Charles VI of France. And many believe that the game is in fact English, and that Charles 1 dedicated the game to his French wife, Henrietta Maria, hence the use of that language to describe play.

Though it has been modernized a great deal over the years, Piquet still enjoys a formal courtly language and set of manners that would certainly lead you to believe that it was invented in a 15th century palace.

Whoever holds the longest sequence, in any suit, wins and a player can score for every sequence in his hand. If the sequences are the same length, then the one with the highest top card wins—if that is the same then there is no score awarded. The scores for sequences are:

- Three cards ("tierce")—3
- Four cards ("quart")—4
- Five cards ("quint") –15
- Six cards ("sixième")—16
- Seven cards ("septième")—17
- Eight cards ("huitième")—18.

Three of a kind or four of a kind, providing it's aces, kings, queens, jacks or tens, score three points (a "trio") and four points (a "quatorze") respectively, for each such meld the holder of the highest has in his hand. If there is a tie, the remaining grouping of the cards of the highest numerical order is the winner.

Players score one point for each trick they have won and one extra point for taking the last trick.

Other bonus scores are as follows:

- For taking seven tricks—10
- For taking all the tricks ("capot")—40
- For the non-dealer scoring 30 points before the dealer scores ("pique")—30
- For scoring 30 points before play begins ("repique")—60

Scores are kept cumulatively on a score sheet.

BETTING

The difference between the winner's and the loser's scores can be translated into a cash value at a pre-arranged rate.

Spit!

PLAYERS: TWO

DECK: ONE

ACES: HIGH OR LOW

SCORE SHEET: YES

SIMPLICITY FACTOR: 7

SKILL FACTOR: 5

SUITABLE FOR CHILDREN: 7

Shuffle and deal so that each player has 26 cards. Each player deals a layout row of five piles. One card for the first pile, two for the second and so on until 5 cards are dealt to the fifth pile. Each player is left with a spit pile of 11 cards, and the object of the game is to play out all their cards to the play piles.

When the players are ready, one says "Spit!" and each takes the top card from his spit pile and puts it face up in the

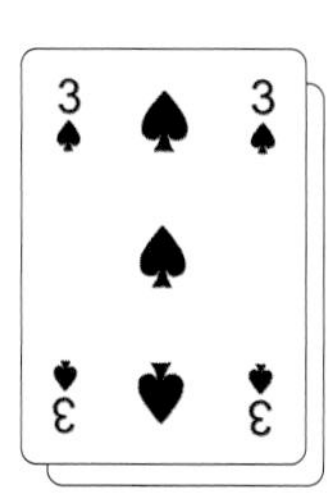

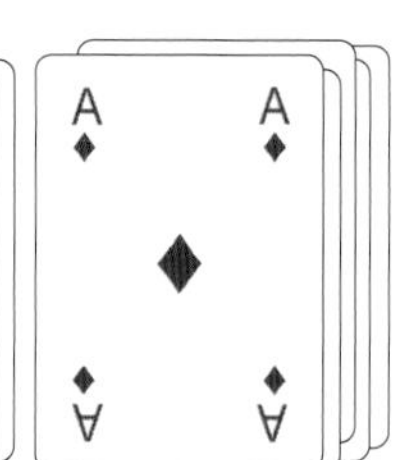

Play piles

Spit pile

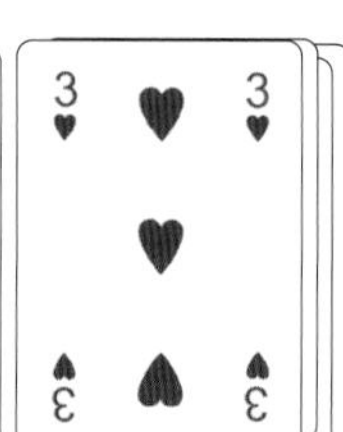

middle of the table. These cards form the play piles. Then, the players begin playing their cards, as fast as they can, from their layout row onto the play piles. Cards can be played if they are one higher or one lower than the top card on the play piles. The suit does not matter, and aces can count as high or low, this means that the sequence can be followed right round from kings, aces and twos.

One hand only can be used in play, and one card can be played at a time. If both players try to play cards to the same pile, the player who puts his card down first wins, the other player must take back his card. Cards played from the layout row can be replaced by a card from the spit pile.

The players play out their cards as fast at they can to the play piles and replace cards in their layout rows. That is, until the players can't play any more cards. Usually between 10 and 15 cards will be played before play stops. When play stops, one player says, "Spit!," and they deal new cards from their spit pile to the play pile they originally started in the middle of the table. Play then continues as before.

When a player has managed to play all the cards in his spit pile, he carries on playing the cards left in his layout row. If play gets stuck after this, only the player with cards left in his spit pile will be able to deal a fresh card to the play piles. When a player has played the last card from his layout row, he is the winner and scores nothing for that round. If both players have played out their spit piles and play stops again, score as below. And play begins again.

SCORING

Score 1 point for each card left in the layout rows and/or spit piles. When one player reaches a score of 100 points, the game is over and the player with the smallest score is the overall winner.

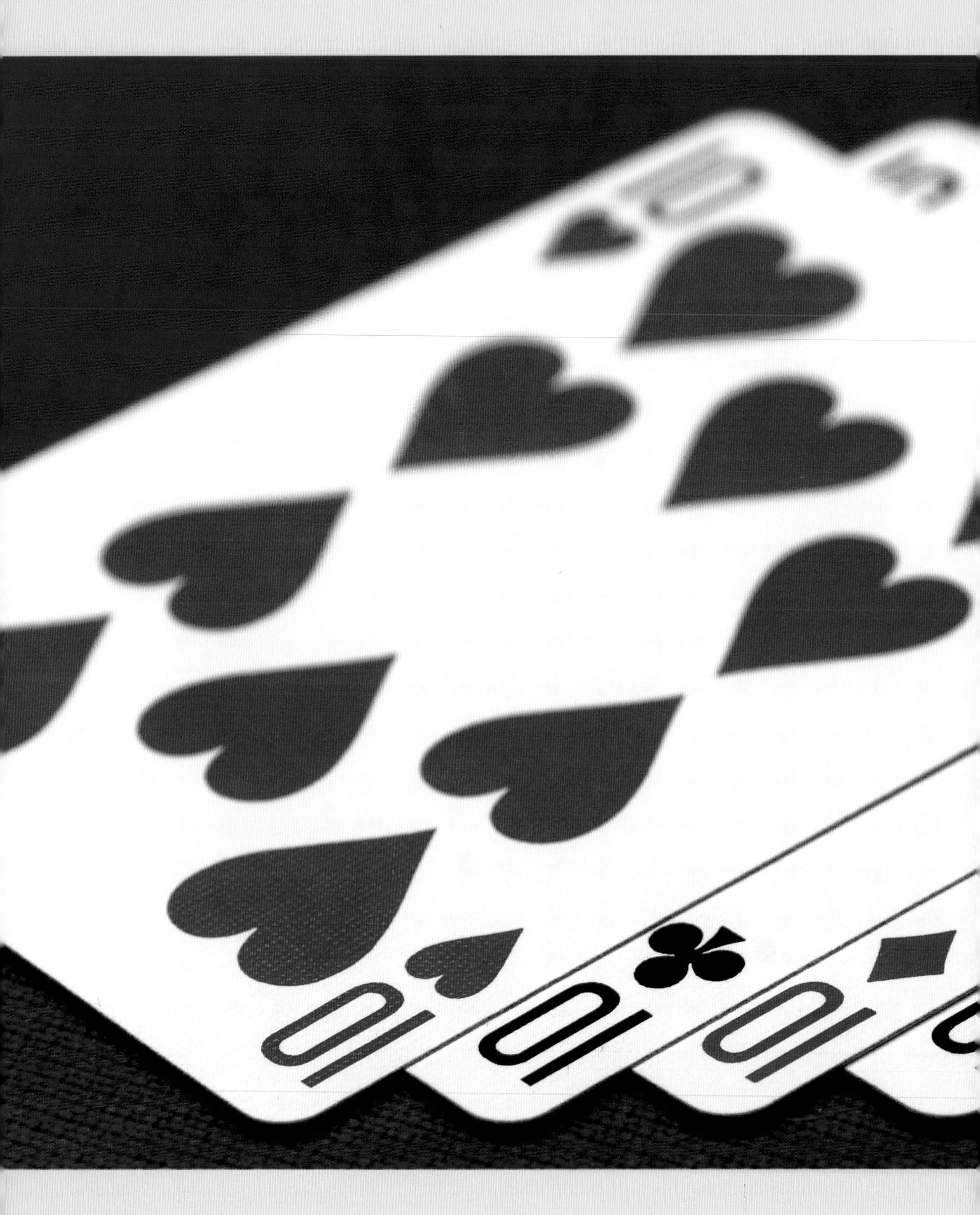

CHAPTER 6

Rummy Games

Probably the most popular card game in the world, Rummy and its variations are universally enjoyed. The aim of the game is basically to make melds or sets of cards (which belong together according to the rules of each game) from your hand. All the games are simple to learn and so are ideal for all ages and most social situations, providing enough to get your brain ticking, without being too intellectually challenging. Canasta is essentially a variation of Rummy played with two decks of cards and two pairs of players—a simple game with a rather complicated scoring system.

Rummy

PLAYERS: TWO TO SIX

DECK: FULL

SCORE SHEET: YES

ACES: HIGH

ORIGIN: USA

SIMPLICITY FACTOR: 4

SKILL FACTOR: 8

SUITABLE FOR CHILDREN: 6

SUITABLE FOR GAMBLING: 4

So named as the game began its life as Rum Poker in the Wild West, Rummy and its variations remain among the most popular card games in the world.

If two players are playing they are dealt 10 cards each; for three or four players, seven cards; for five or six, six cards. Undealt cards are placed in a face-down stack on the table, with the top of this stack turned face-up and placed next to it.

The players' aim is to "meld" their hands into sets of three or four of a kind, or sequences of four cards or more in the

The king wins

A short history of Rummy

The majority of evidence suggests that various games with similarities to Rummy first appeared in China. The Rummy principles of drawing and discarding with the aim of melding cards into sets appear in many different Chinese card games from around the 18th century. The classic Chinese game Mahjong, played with a set of tiles of various designs, is similar to Rummy in that it involves picking up and discarding tiles until one player has a hand of winning combinations.

Gin Rummy is said to have been devised in 1909 by a Whist teacher called Elwood T. Baker of Brooklyn, New York. It was a hugely popular card game in the United States throughout the 1940s and continues to be a popular family card game today. Gin rummy became something of a craze among actors on Broadway and in Hollywood in the 1940s and it was mentioned, and even featured in, many films at the time. Its popularity may be attributed to the fact that is fast to play but can easily be stopped at short notice and the hands taken up again as soon as the players are free. Thus making it the ideal game to play on a film set.

same suit. They do this by, in turn, exchanging single cards in their hands for cards on the table. Players can take either the top card of the face-down stack or the upturned card.

They then discard any card from their hand on to the face-up pile. Unless a player is going for "rummy"—all the cards in their hand in sequence—once melds are made they are placed face-up in front of the player who made them and all players are free to add cards to each other's melds at any time during the game. The winner is the first player to get rid of all their cards either by calling "rummy" or by placing them on theirs or other players' melds.

SCORING

Once a player has dropped out, the denominations of each other player's hand is

totaled (picture cards count as 10, aces as one). If the winning player has made rummy, the totals of every other hand in that particular round are doubled. The overall winner is the player with the least number of points to their name at the end of the prescribed time.

BETTING

A cash-for-points system is the best way to approach this, and if there are more than two players, it would help if one of them was a mathematician.

Variations

GIN RUMMY

A version for two players, who are dealt 10 cards each and aim to go "Gin" by arranging all of those cards in one sequence. No early melds are allowed.

KNOCK RUMMY

A version of Gin Rummy that is ended early if a player knocks the table after he has picked up a card but before he discards. Both players then meld as many cards as possible (there is no adding to the opponent's melds) and add up the scores of their remainders. If the knocker is lower, he scores the difference plus 10; if the knocker is beaten, the knockee scores the difference plus 25.

BOATHOUSE RUMMY

Here if players take from the face-up pile they must take from the face-down pile too, yet only discard one card. There are no melds in this version and to win a player must go rummy with the entire hand.

MICHIGAN RUMMY

This version sees the face-up pile spread out so a player can take a card that was discarded a while ago, provided they take all the cards on top of it. This card must then immediately be put down in a meld or added to an existing one. Scoring is back to front here, with players earning points for the melds they put down, and the winner of each hand gaining the points from the cards the other players are left holding. Aces can be high or low and count as 15 points for those left in opponents' hands or as one point if at the end of a low end meld (four, three, two, ace).

CONTINENTAL RUMMY

Here two decks of cards are shuffled together. Each player is dealt 15 cards (this can be done in threes). Three-or four-of-a-kind melds are not permitted and cards must be arranged in numerical sequences of three or more. No melds are laid down early, and to win players must meld their entire hand into one of the following combinations: five melds of three cards; three of four cards and one of three or one five, a four and two threes. Jokers are wild, aces can be high or low and scoring is the same as in regular Rummy.

Canasta

PLAYERS: TWO PAIRS

DECK: TWO

SCORE SHEET: YES

ORIGIN: SOUTH AMERICA

SIMPLICITY FACTOR: 3

SKILL FACTOR: 7

SUITABLE FOR CHILDREN: 2

SUITABLE FOR GAMBLING: 8

Essentially a variation of Rummy, Canasta is played with two decks, all the jokers and two pairs of players seated opposite each other. Suits are irrelevant in Canasta, as cards are matched by denomination only.

Eleven cards are dealt to each player. The remaining deck is put in the middle of the table, face-down with the top card upturned and placed next to the pile to start a face-up discard stack, known as "the pot". In turn, players take the top card from the face-down stack, absorb it into their hand and discard one on to the pot. Players are attempting to make "melds" by laying sets of three or more cards of the same denomination face-up in front of them.

Points are scored in running team totals for each card laid down. New cards can be added to a player's or his partner's melds (but not their opponents') at any stage during the game. The hand is won as soon as a player gets rid of all of his cards. However, a player cannot put down all his cards until he and his partner have made a "canasta" by melding seven of the same denomination cards. Jokers and deuces can be used as wild cards to make the canasta but there are the following limits to the number of wild cards used in a meld: one in a three-card meld, two in a four-card meld and three in five or over (including a canasta).

At any time, players may pick up the entire pot instead of a card from the face-down pile. While these extra cards may be necessary for them to make a canasta, it can also give them many other cards to have to meld. (In some variations of canasta, the pot cannot be taken up unless that player's team

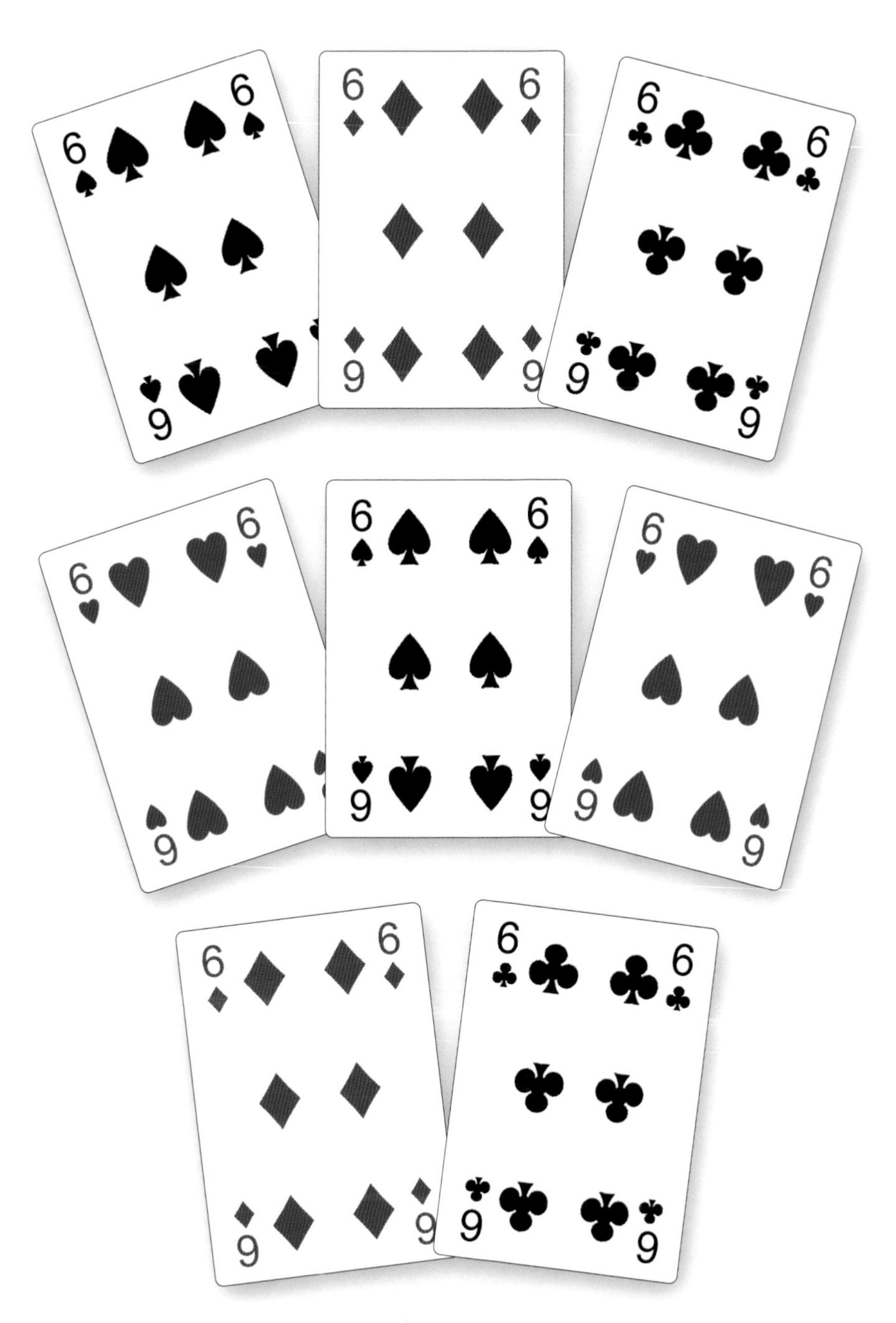

A canasta

has already made a meld of 50 points or more, or can use the top card on the pot as part of a meld that doesn't involve a wild card.)

Games are usually won by the first pair to make 5,000 points.

SCORING

Canasta's scoring system is what makes essentially a simple game suddenly very complicated. Scores are awarded to the players for the cards they've laid down in melds and added to the score sheet as the melds are made.

The wild cards—jokers and deuces—regardless of what they are used to represent, are worth 50 and 20 points respectively; king, queen, jack, ten, nine and eight all score ten each; seven, six, five and four all score five.

A short history of Canasta

Canasta means basket in Spanish and there are many different theories about how it came by its name. It may refer to the fact that the object of the game is to collect points by making melds, or sets, of three of more cards. Or the name may have come about because of the tray that was originally used to hold the stock and the discards.

The game of Canasta is said to have been invented in Montevideo, the capital of Uruguay in the 1940s. The story goes that the ladies of Montevideo were so fed up with the amount of time their men spent playing poker, that they devised the game try to attract them away from the poker tables.

From there Canasta spread from card table to card table until it reached North America, and soon became a popular game all over the world. In the 1950s Canasta even threatened to topple Bridge as the world's most fashionable game. And its success with the British royal family sealed its popularity.

Canasta is still a widely-played game today but the many variations of the game enjoyed now are very different to the original South American version.

Threes are special: red threes are placed face-up as soon as a player gets one, a replacement card is drawn and each scores 100 points. If a player is dealt all four red threes and places them down together the bonus is 800. Black threes cannot be melded except by a player going out, they only count for five points and should be discarded immediately.

Canastas score bonus points as well as the cards' total: a "natural canasta" (no wild cards) earns 500 bonus points, a "mixed canasta" (involving wild cards) scores 300. A hundred points are awarded to the team that wins, while that can be doubled if a player goes out "concealed" by melding his entire 11 cards without making any previous melds. After a team has won, the points value of the losers' unmelded cards is totaled up and subtracted from their existing score.

BETTING

Points for cash—a prearranged value—with the difference between the two team scores at the end constituting the "pot".

Variations

In Two-Handed Canasta each player has 15 cards and must make two canastas before going out. Three-Handed Canasta is played with 13 cards and two canastas. Six-Handed Canasta involves three decks, two teams of three seated opposite each other, two canastas to end a hand and is played up to 10,000 points, with a meld of five red threes being worth 1,000 points and all six 1,200. Cutthroat Canasta is a variation of Three-Handed Canasta in which if a player takes the pot, the other two immediately become a team against him.

CHAPTER 7

Five-Card Games

These games are usually grouped together because they are played in similar ways and have evolved from the same family of French games, not because they literally involve a hand of five cards. Ecartre used to be popular in French casinos and involves side-betting and a rather complicated scoring system. Euchre is speedy to play once the initial trumping and bidding is out of the way. Five hundred is similar to Euchre, it originated in the USA and is now very popular in Australia. Napoleon is a great gambling game with an interesting Battle of Waterloo scoring system.

Five Hundred

PLAYERS: TWO TO FIVE

SCORE SHEET: YES

DECK: SEVEN UPWARDS PLUS ONE JOKER

ACES: HIGH

ORIGIN: USA

SIMPLICITY FACTOR: 9

SKILL FACTOR: 7

SUITABLE FOR CHILDREN: 3

SUITABLE FOR GAMBLING: 6

Very similar to Euchre, with elements of Pinochle, this 100-year-old game is essentially a three-hander, but has variations that can involve up to five players. It is one of the very few card games in which spades is not the highest-ranked suit.

It is played with a 33-card deck that features nothing lower than a seven, but with the addition of a joker. The joker becomes the most valuable card in whichever suit is trumps (it is known as the "best bower"), followed by, as in Euchre, the jack of trumps (the "right bower") and then the jack of the same color (the "left bower").

Ten cards are dealt to each player, in two parcels of three and one of four. A "widow" parcel of three is put aside between the first and second round of dealing.

The most valuable cards in Five Hundred

TRUMPS	6 TRICKS	7 TRICKS	8 TRICKS	9 TRICKS	10 TRICKS
SPADES	40	140	240	340	440
CLUBS	60	160	260	360	460
DIAMONDS	80	180	280	380	480
HEARTS	100	200	300	400	500
NO TRUMPS	120	220	320	420	520

Auction-style bidding then begins as the three players declare how many tricks they think they can take with whatever suit they call as trumps, or without trumps. As the auction progresses upward, each bid is called a "jump". Players can pass if they want to and if all three pass, the hand is void, the deal passes to the left and the cards are shuffled and re-dealt. There is a progressive value of bids (see the table above) running from six tricks with spades as trumps (40) to ten tricks with no trumps (520). The highest bidder takes up the unseen widow cards, and discards any three cards he chooses. He then leads for the first trick.

Tricks are played for as normal and, although the contract winner is now effectively playing against the other two players, they will both count their scores separately.

Scores are kept cumulatively from hand to hand and the winner is the first to 500. Hence the name. If more than one player reaches 500 in the same hand, then whoever won that contract takes preference, or if there is no contract winner involved it's the player who got there first.

SCORING

If the contract winner makes his contract he scores the number of points it is worth (see the above box). If he doesn't the same amount will be deducted from his total, which could result in a minus figure.

Each of the two non-contract winners scores 10 points for each trick they take. If the contract is for less than nine tricks but the contract winner makes all ten, then he scores 250 points on top of the value of the contract.

Variations

TWO-HANDED FIVE HUNDRED

Played to the same rules, with the same number of cards. Three hands are dealt but the third one is left face-down while the two players play out the hand.

FOUR-HANDED FIVE HUNDRED

Two pairs compete against each other and score together. The deck includes the sixes, fives and red fours. Apart from that, the rules are essentially the same.

FIVE-HANDED FIVE HUNDRED

A full deck including the joker is used to make 53 (five hands of ten and a three-card widow). The successful contract bidder can choose a partner by nominating a specific card and whoever has it has to play with him against the other three.

Euchre

PLAYERS: TWO TO FOUR

SCORE SHEET: YES

DECK: NO CARDS BELOW A SEVEN

ACES: HIGH

ORIGIN: FRANCE

SIMPLICITY FACTOR: 8

SKILL FACTOR: 6

SUITABLE FOR CHILDREN: 3

SUITABLE FOR GAMBLING: 5

A quick and straight-to-the-point game, Euchre was once the most popular trumps game in the USA, although its origins are French. Speedy as the actual game is, however, there are certain conventions that have to be established before play can begin. Euchre can be played with two, three or four players, but, as it is the most straightforward, the two-player game is explained here.

The deck features no cards lower than a seven and aces are high unless in the trump suit. In that case, the highest value card is the jack of trumps (known as "the right bower") with the jack of the same color ("the left bower") being the second highest in the deck, then the trump suit runs down as normal—ace, king, queen, ten, nine and so on.

Each player is dealt five cards, as a three and a two, then the next card of the remainder is turned face-up to signify trumps. If the non-dealer reckons he can make at least three tricks with that suit as trumps, but with the dealer having that particular trump (the turned-up card) in his hand, he announces "I'll take it up", and the dealer discards a card to take up the turned-up card. If he doesn't believe he can make that many tricks with that suit as trumps he says "I'll pass". The dealer then gets the chance to "bid", which he does in exactly the same way, taking up the upturned card if he accepts that suit as trumps. When the dealer decides to take it up or pass, he is doing so in the knowledge that the upturned card will be part of his hand.

If both players pass on this first round of bidding, the non-dealer can nominate any suit he likes as trumps if he thinks

he can thus take at least three tricks. If he passes, the dealer has the same opportunity. If they both pass, the hands are folded and the cards are dealt again.

The object is to take as many tricks as possible in the conventional manner—the non-dealer or the winner of the last trick leads, the highest card in that suit or trump (with the right and left bowers being the highest cards) takes the trick. The object is to take as many tricks as possible. Scoring takes place at the end of each hand.

Games are played to the first player reaching a pre-agreed total (usually seven, nine or ten) from a series of hands or the most points after a set number of games.

SCORING

- Each trick won—1.
- Either player taking three or four tricks—1.
- The player who called trumps not taking three tricks (he is "euchred")—2 points subtracted.
- Either player taking five tricks (a "march")—2.

A right bower and a left bower

BETTING

A cash-for-points system, paid on the differences between the scores at the end of the game, is the obvious method.

Variations

CUTTHROAT EUCHRE

The rules are the same for this three-handed version as for the two-handed game, so the player who calls trumps has to make his march against two other players. Three points are awarded for a march, but when a player is euchred both his opponents gain two points.

FOUR-HANDED EUCHRE

Four players play as two partnerships sitting opposite each other. The rules are the same, but, during the bidding process, if the dealer's partner wants to let the dealer know he wants the suit of the face-up card as trumps he announces "I assist", and the dealer will know to take it up. The other partnership has no such privileges, and their taking up those trumps will still put the face-up card into the dealer's hand. Although players play individually, their scores are totaled up as a partnership, and the scoring is as for the two-handed game. However, the player who bids trumps can declare they are "going it alone", at which point their partner folds his hand and the game continues as for three-handed euchre.

AUCTION EUCHRE

This is played by two partnerships, but without the turned-up trump. Each player bids for how many tricks they think they could make—three, four or five—with their as yet undeclared choice of trumps. The highest bid wins the right to chose trumps and if the bidding team makes that number of tricks, they score that many points. If they are euchred, the other team scores the amount bid.

Ecartre

PLAYERS: TWO

SCORE SHEET: NO

DECK: NO CARDS BELOW A SEVEN

ACES: HIGH

ORIGIN: FRANCE

SIMPLICITY FACTOR: 5

SKILL FACTOR: 7

SUITABLE FOR CHILDREN: 4

SUITABLE FOR GAMBLING: 5

Ecartre is a game that used to be very popular in French casinos, where it always attracted a good deal of side-betting and had a very complicated scoring system of penalties and bonuses. The game described here is the domestic version, which is much more straightforward. That said, the scoring system still seems disproportionate to the actual play.

Using a piquet deck (no cards below a seven), two players are dealt five cards each with the next card turned up to determine trumps. If the non-dealer decides he can win three tricks he announces he will play and the game commences, playing for tricks by going higher in the same suit or

A hand worth proposing

trumping. If he doesn't think he can make three tricks, he will "propose" and if it is "accepted" by the dealer, he can discard any number of cards from his hand and be dealt new ones. The dealer can then do the same.

If the dealer opts not to accept the proposal, the game is played without exchanging any cards. Each hand continues until all five tricks are won, points are cumulative from hand to hand, and the deal changes after each hand.

SCORING

- If the card turned up for trumps is a king, the dealer scores 1.
- If either player wins three or four tricks they score 1.
- Taking all five tricks is called a vole and earns 2.
- If either player has made three or four tricks when there was no proposal, or the proposal was refused, he wins an extra point. (In each of these cases, it's still only two points for making all five.)
- The winner is the first player to five points.

BETTING

Away from the obvious attractions of side-betting, it's best just to settle up at the end of each game with the difference between the players' scores determining what is paid out.

Napoleon

PLAYERS: TWO TO SIX
DECK: FULL
SCORE SHEET: NO
ORIGIN: ENGLAND
SIMPLICITY FACTOR: 9
SKILL FACTOR: 7
SUITABLE FOR CHILDREN: 5
SUITABLE FOR GAMBLING: 9

In spite of the name, this is an English card game. It was very popular in the late 18th and early 19th centuries, and remains interesting thanks to its singular scoring system, which is based on what went on at the Battle of Waterloo.

Between two and six players are dealt five cards each from a full deck and bid as to how many tricks they think they can make, with the highest bid choosing trumps. Players can pass or bid "Nullo"—to take no tricks. The game is then continued as for Whist, with the player who won the contract effectively playing against the rest. Once all the tricks have been played, the scores are added up.

Napoleon is a game of probabilities and judgement, and experience usually pays off. As a general rule it is as well to get rid of likely losing cards as soon as you can.

Did you know?

Napoleon, or Nap as it is often known, is a card game of experience and judgement, which seems apt given that it is named after Napoleon Bonaparte (1769-1821), a brilliant general and Emperor of France from 1804-1815. His Code Napoleon remains the basis of French Law to this day.

The Duke of Wellington was the English general who finally defeated Emperor Napoleon at the Battle of Waterloo in 1815. And Blucher was a Prussian Field Marshall who played a key role in the French defeat at Waterloo.

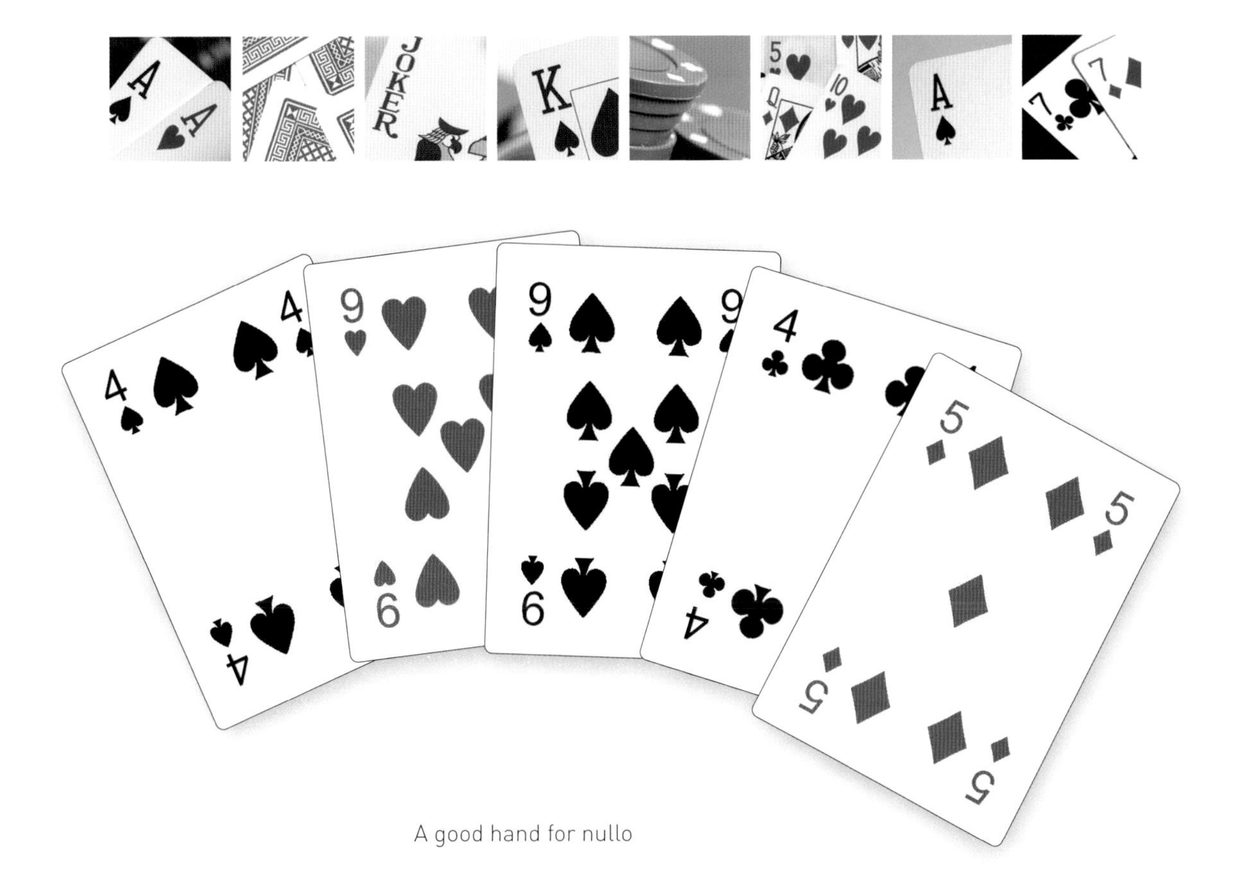

A good hand for nullo

SCORING

If the contracted player makes his contract, he wins that number of points, unless the bid was for all five (a "Napoleon") which wins five points and a bonus of five or it is a bid of nullo, which wins three points.

BETTING

Napoleon is an ideal game for gambling, each player should hold a stack of chips and a more involved scoring system can be applied, as follows. Successful contracts mean each player pays the winner that number of chips—including three for nullo. On a successful Napoleon, the winner is paid double by each player (10 chips) but only need pay each out singly if he loses. If the contract is for a Napoleon, the bidder has the chance to declare "Wellington" which doubles the stakes to 20 for a win and a payout of 10 for a loss. Then there is a "Blucher" which triples the bid to 30 for a win and 15 paid out for a loss. Wellingtons and Bluchers can be used if two players have bid Napoleons, with the higher winning the contract.

CHAPTER 8

Banking Games

These games differ from other gambling games in that the players play against the dealer or banker, and very often the dealer has the advantage. Pontoon is probably the most widely played and popular game of this type and is also known as Blackjack or Twenty-one. The aim of the game is to bet on a hand that adds up to twenty-one, or near to it. Baccarat is similar but the players are aiming for a hand of eight or nine, which is known as a natural. Red Dog is a fast, exciting game where the stakes can mount up very quickly.

Baccarat

PLAYERS: ANY
DECK: UP TO THREE
SCORE SHEET: NO
ACES: LOW
ORIGIN: ITALY OR FRANCE
SIMPLICITY FACTOR: 7
SKILL FACTOR: 7
SUITABLE FOR CHILDREN: 7

A casino-based, players-against-the-bank-type game that won't be much fun if you're not betting on it. Using three decks shuffled together, the banker deals two cards, face-down and individually, to each of the players, including himself as the last in the round. Players examine their cards then place their bets against the bank, who plays against each player separately.

Players have to add their cards up to a score of eight or nine, using a scoring system that has an ace valued as one, the pictures worth no points and the other cards scoring their number. If any of the players have a "natural"—a total of eight or nine from their original two cards—and the dealer doesn't, they win and are paid out. If the two cards add up to more than ten, only the last digit will be used, for instance a hand of seven and nine would be added together to make sixteen and would count as six.

A natural nine

If nobody has a natural, players will be dealt further cards, face-up, and continue trying to make a total of eight or nine without going over. Once they stop, the dealer deals his own hand—with all cards face-up—to try to get closer to eight or nine than he thinks his opponents are, without going over the top.

SCORING

If a player and the banker both get cards adding up to eight or nine, nine wins out over eight. If a player gets the same score as the bank—either in a natural or otherwise—the bets are off.

BETTING

The limit for wagers should be pre-set. If cards are dealt beyond the original two, then the stake can be increased before the turn of each new card.

Variations

Chemin-de-fer is the most popular variation of Baccarat, in which the dealer only plays against the player who has made the biggest bet, with the others having the choice to bet alongside that player or drop out.

A short history of Baccarat

Baccarat (pronounced "bac-car-ah") is an ancient gambling game and an early version was played with cards from a Tarot deck as far back as the Middle Ages. The modern variation probably originated in Italy around 1490, and today is most likely to be seen in European casinos.

The word baccarat comes from the Italian word *baccara*, which means zero, and refers to the zero value given to all of the face cards and tens.

In the 1550s, its popularity spread to France where aristocrats were looking for a new and fast-moving game of chance. They renamed it "chemin de fer" which means railroad.

Chemin de fer then travelled from Europe to South American and found a new home in Argentina, where wealthy South Americans flocked to the gambling paradise of Mar Del Plata. The game travelled on to Cuba, where the rules were adapted and it became American Baccarat (in the American version each player bets against the house, in the original Chemin de Fer the players bet among themselves).

Pontoon

PLAYERS: ANY

DECK: FULL

SCORE SHEET: NO

ACES: HIGH AND LOW

ORIGIN: EUROPE

SIMPLICITY FACTOR: 6

SKILL FACTOR: 8

SUITABLE FOR CHILDREN: 7

SUITABLE FOR GAMBLING: 10

What follows is the domestic version of the casino game often called Blackjack (in the USA) or Twenty-one. It can be played by any number of players, each of whom is individually playing against the bank, i.e. the dealer. The idea of the game is to get a hand that adds up to 21, or as close to it as possible, preferably in just two cards.

The dealer deals each player one card, face-down. Players look at their card and put down a bet depending on its value. Once betting is complete, the banker looks at his card and, if he chooses, can then ask the players, en masse, to double their wagers. Any who don't wish to must drop out and lose their stake.

Each player, and the bank, is then dealt a second card. Any player with a "pontoon"—an ace and a picture card or a ten—turns his cards face-up to declare it. If there are no pontoons among the players' hands, the players will, in turn, start playing against the bank by announcing they will "twist" or "stick". If a player twists, the dealer deals him a face-up card and the player takes it into his hand. If that hand is still sufficiently short of 21 to warrant another card, they will twist again. Once they are satisfied with the total, they say they will stick, and the dealer moves on to the next player to repeat the process. If a player's total exceeds 21, they are "bust", must fold their hand and the dealer takes their stake.

After all the players have finished, the dealer turns over his cards and plays his hand in the same way. If the dealer has a pontoon, he beats every other hand—even other pontoons, as in the event of a tie the dealer has the advantage—and

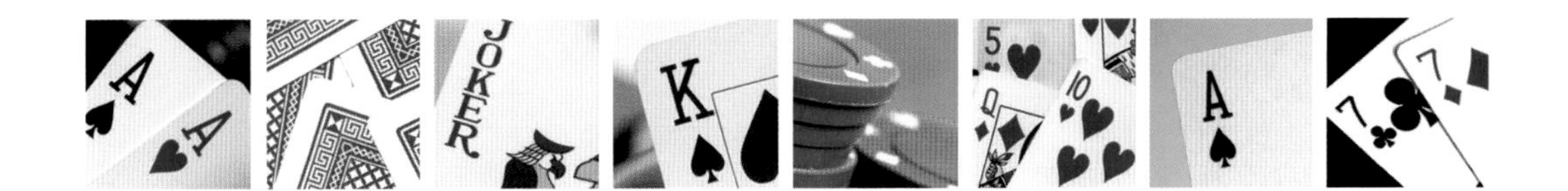

takes in all the stake money. If he doesn't and another player does, he pays that player the value of his stake and then commences to play against the rest. If any player has twisted three times and remains below 21 it is a "five-card trick" and the actual value only counts if the dealer has a five-card trick too, then the lowest total wins. Otherwise, players that have totals closer to 21 than the dealer achieves get paid their stake, those that don't lose.

Players who are dealt two cards the same in the original deal have the option to "split"—they are dealt one more card to each of those held, and play each as a separate hand against the dealer, repeating the original stake. When a player makes pontoon, providing the dealer doesn't, he takes over the deal from the next hand.

SCORING

Aces can count as 11 or as one, depending on what works best for the player; picture cards are ten; everything else counts at face value. A pontoon beats everything, a five-card trick is second best and after that it's whichever totals are nearest to 21 without going bust.

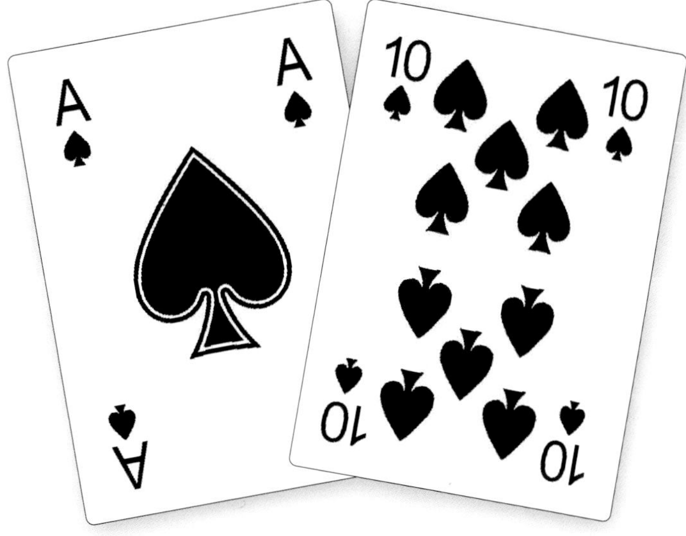

The classic pontoon

Red Dog

PLAYERS: THREE OR MORE

DECK: FULL

SCORE SHEET: NO

ACES: HIGH

ORIGIN: USA

SIMPLICITY FACTOR: 8

SKILL FACTOR: 9

SUITABLE FOR CHILDREN: 0

SUITABLE FOR GAMBLING: 10

A fast-moving, rather exciting gambling game that belies its apparent simplicity as the stakes involved can quickly mount up.

Each player puts a specified amount into the pot, then each is dealt five cards from a full deck, with the remainder put face-down in the centre of the table. In turn, from the dealer's left, each player bets that they can beat the top card of the deck (which has yet to be turned over) with a card from their hand. The minimum bet is one unit and the maximum is the entire pot. The card is then revealed and the players have to beat it by showing a higher card in the same suit.

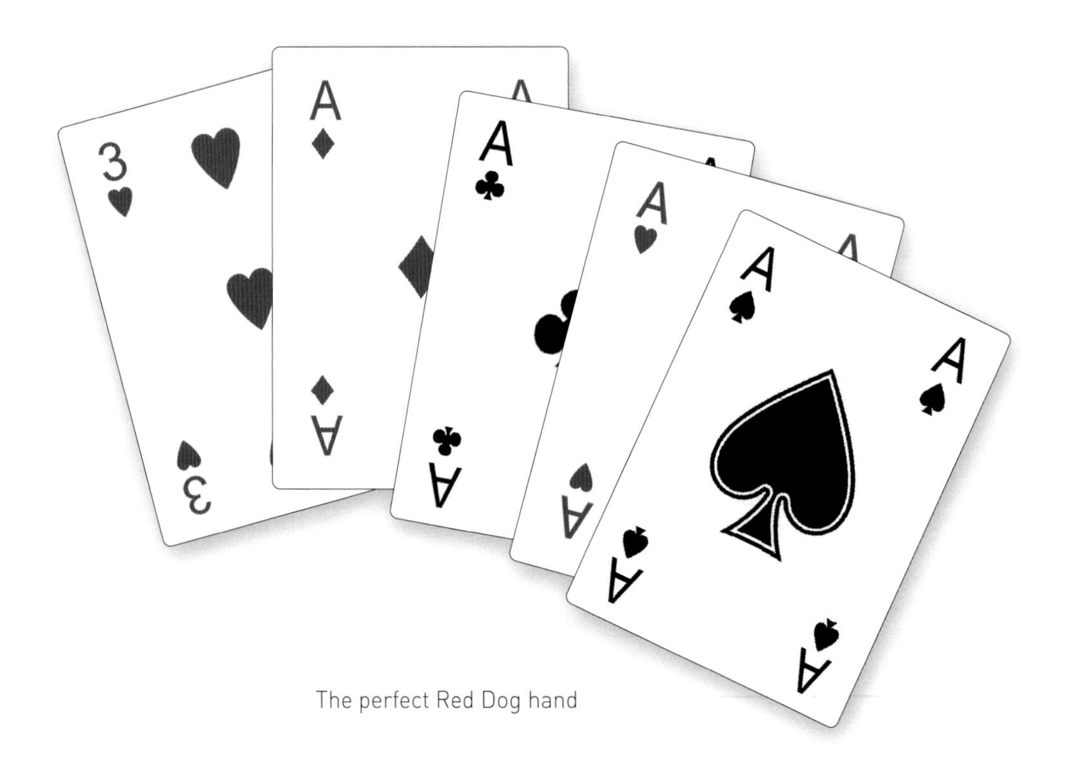

The perfect Red Dog hand

If they can, they show the winning card only and take the amount wagered from the pot; if not their stake goes into the pot and they don't show their cards. As the value of the pot can change during a round of play, a player who bets "the pot" wins or loses the amount that is in it at the end of that round. If more than one player bets "the pot" and is successful in the same round, they share between them, equally, whatever is in the pot at the end of that round.

After a round has been played, the turned-up card is put face-down on the bottom of the deck, as are the players' thrown in hands, and the deal is passed to the left. Whatever is in the pot from game to game is left there, which means it can build up to quite a sum if a few unsuccessful big bets are made. If it is won, then the players contribute again to a new one.

Variations

THREE-CARD RED DOG

This is the version of the game usually played in casinos. It is not possible to hold one card in every suit and the "perfect Red Dog hand" of four aces cannot be held by any player.

Did you know?

As with most card games there are many different opinions about the rules of Red Dog and even about its correct name. It sometimes goes by the name of High Card Pool, and has a number of other popular casino variations such as Slippery Sam and Shoot.

In US casinos the name Red Dog is also sometimes used for another gambling game where two cards are dealt and the bets are laid on whether the next card will rank between the first two cards. This is also known as Ace-Deuce or In Between.

CHAPTER 9

Poker

First known by name in around 1829, Poker is thought to have originated in New Orleans. It travelled to Victorian England in the 1850s and has gone from strength to strength ever since. The combination of luck, card-playing skills and intuition makes poker one of the most difficult but fascinating card games. This section provides an introduction to one of the world's most popular card games, and gives the low-down on basic rules and betting. It then goes on to deal with three of the more popular poker variations in some detail—providing a wealth of expert hints and tips on play, strategy and bluffing.

Poker

PLAYERS: UP TO TEN
DECK: FULL (USUALLY)
SCORE SHEET: NO
ACES: HIGH
ORIGIN: USA
SIMPLICITY FACTOR: 2
SKILL FACTOR: 10
SUITABLE FOR CHILDREN: 2
SUITABLE FOR GAMBLING: 10

Poker is one of the great mind sports, along with chess and bridge, and is probably one of the most difficult games to play well. Chess is a game of total information in which your skill lies in your superior deductive reasoning. Poker is mainly a game of inadequate information where you must assess the actions and probable reactions of your opponents. Bridge lies somewhere in between and differs from the other two in being a partnership game. Many players try all three and, in fact, quite a number become expert in at least two of them.

Poker has long been a really popular card game in the U.S., and has only recently caught on in Britain and Europe. Of course it does have a somewhat sleazy reputation, some of it undoubtedly deserved.

There is a myriad of poker variations and each poker player has their favorite. Poker is what might be described as a living game, in that it has changed and developed throughout its history, and will in all probability continue to do so.

The basic rules of poker are fairly straightforward but, like Bridge, there are so many subtleties involved in the playing and betting that literally hundreds of books have been written on the subject. So what follows here is how to play, score and bet in a very basic way. After that, it's entirely up to the individual player how far they want to develop their skills in this fascinating game. There are plenty of simple, fun variations for playing poker at home, but you will not see any of these games being played in casinos.

As well as basic rules and betting, there is a brief outline of

a few of the more commonplace examples such as Straight Poker and Five-Card Stud. And after that, there are three sections focussing on the classic poker games: Texas Hold 'em, Omaha and Seven Card Stud. These sections provide a comprehensive breakdown of the intricacies of play and strategy, with plenty of useful hints and tips from Stewart Reuben, who has been a professional poker player for nearly 40 years. Each section will take you step by step through each game, from the initial deal. There are analyses of individual sample hands, an in-depth look at betting and a question and answer format to help you develop your poker skills even further. Finally, there is a short section on the finer points of play—bluffing, categories of player and odds.

When twos are wild—which will be decided on at the start of a game—the highest hand is five of a kind, which is four of a kind and a two. If a wild two is used against a "natural hand"—one that has made the same combination without recourse to a two—the natural takes preference.

A royal flush

Basic rules

From two to ten players can take part in a game of poker. To follow are the basic rules, but more specific rules applying to Texas Hold 'em, Seven Card Stud and Omaha are listed on their respective introduction pages.

• Essentially each player receives five cards. There are many variations of poker, but the basic principle always remains the same. The winner, of a particular *hand*, is the person who has the best five cards, or is the only person still in the *pot*.

• The players wager on who has the best hand. Bets go into the pot.

• In most forms of poker, an Ace counts as either the highest card, or lowest, at the option of the player.

• The suits do not matter. Two hands which are identical in face value, but in different suits, count the same and share the pot.

The table opposite shows the names of the hands, their order of merit and the number of possible ways each hand can be dealt from the 52-card deck.

There are many technical words and terms in poker.

Each time one of these terms first appears in the text it is italicized.

The explanations are listed in poker terms, starting on page 197.

Name	Examples	Possible hands
Royal flush	A♣K♣Q♣J♣10♣ A♠K♠Q♠J♠10♠ Sharing the pot.	4
Straight flush	9♥8♥7♥6♥5♥ 5♦4♦3♦2♦A♦ The highest ranked card in the sequence is the winner. A 9 high straight flush beats a 5 high one.	36
Four of a kind, known in some places as poker.	8♠8♦8♥8♣2♣ 5♦5♥5♠5♣K♥	624
Full house	J♣J♠J♥K♠K♥ Q♠Q♣Q♥2♠2♦ The higher ranking three of a kind is the winner	3,744
Flush	A♦J♦9♦8♦2♦ A♠J♠7♠6♠5♠ The first hand beats the second because the third card is higher.	5,108
Straight	K♥Q♥J♥10♦9♥ 7♠6♦5♥4♣3♣	10,200
Three of a kind, also known as a prile or trips.	8♣8♥8♦3♥2♠ 3♦3♣3♠A♥K♠	54,912
Two pair	J♥J♣2♠2♦4♥ 10♠10♦9♠9♦A♣ 10♥10♣9♣9♥J♣ The first hand is best as the Jacks are higher. The second hand beats the third as the fifth card is higher.	123,552
One pair	8♣8♠Q♦7♠6♥ 6♦6♠A♥K♦Q♠	1,098,240
No pair	K♠J♦10♥7♦5♠ J♥9♠8♣6♥4♠	1,302,540
TOTAL from a 52-card *deck*.		**2,598,960**

Some common forms of poker

In its early forms, Poker was a much more simple game than it is now. It was played with just one straightforward round of betting, hence the name Straight Poker. The players were dealt five cards and then the betting began. Over time, the game was gradually modified and draw poker developed—the draw giving players the chance to trade in one or more of their cards for a new one. These modifications, and others such as wild cards and bluffing, essentially came about to give the professional gamblers a chance to win more money. There are many different variations on the basic game of poker, and here we run through some of the more common forms.

STRAIGHT POKER

Players are singly dealt a hand of five cards each, and play that through the rounds of betting, with no chance to change any of them. Once everybody has finished betting, the hands are compared and the highest takes the pot.

DRAW POKER

Players are singly dealt a hand of five cards each, and a round of betting takes place in which players can drop out. Once that is finished, starting on the dealer's left and moving round the table, each player has the opportunity to discard as many cards as they want and "draw" (get dealt) fresh ones from the deck. Then another round of betting takes place, in which players are again free to drop out. Once that is over, the remaining players compare hands.

FIVE-CARD STUD

Most popular in the U.S., this is the game that the most daring poker players go for. It involves more nerve and judgment than draw poker as everybody can see four of the cards in every player's hands.

Each player is dealt a card face-down and then a card face-up. They inspect their face-down card and leave it hidden, then the player with the highest face-up card

opens the betting, or folds his hand. After that round of betting every player left in is dealt another face-up card and the player with the highest scoring cards showing opens the next round of betting. The same process is repeated twice more until every player still in the game has four face-up cards and one, his "hole card", face-down. The betting now goes round the table once more before the players reveal their hole cards to make their hands.

STRIPPED DECK POKER

This is Draw or Five-Card Stud where there are only three or four players and the low cards—twos to fives—are removed from the deck. This obviously increases the chances of getting high-scoring hands.

WILD CARD POKER

Exactly what it says, this is any game of poker in which it has been agreed beforehand that one denomination of card—usually the deuces—can count as any other card.

When deuces/twos are wild the highest hand is five of a kind, which is four of a kind and a two. If a wild two is used against a "natural hand"—one that has made the same combination without recourse to a two—the natural takes preference.

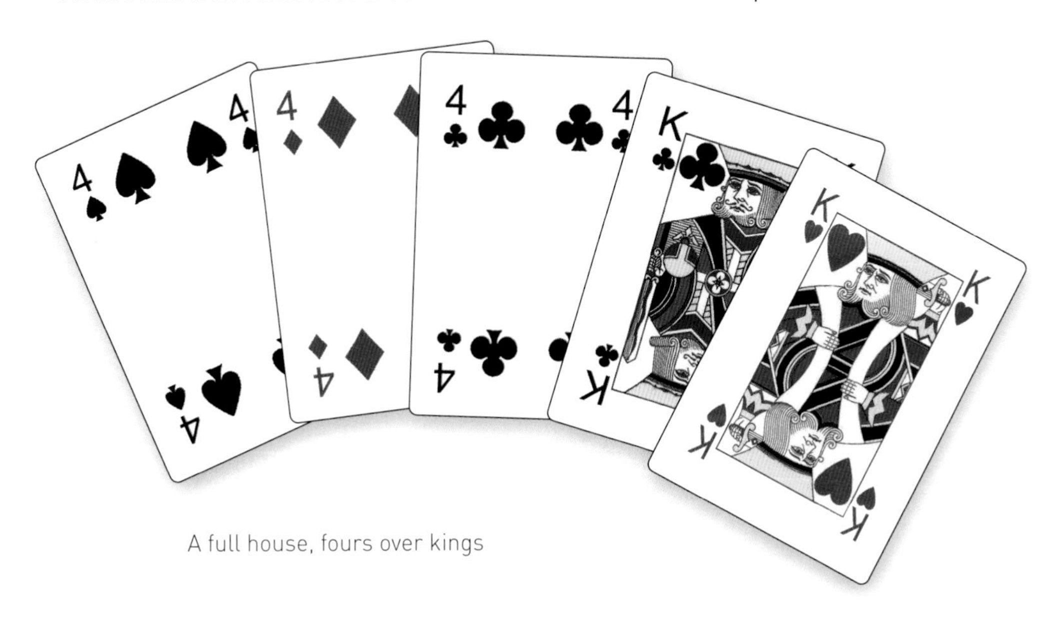

A full house, fours over kings

The betting system

It is not compulsory to play poker for money. Playing with matchsticks is a good way to start, and M&Ms would be an excellent alternative. In fact on most Internet sites, you can play for "play money". And this is because it is a good idea to familiarize yourself with the game in some detail using chips or tokens to start with. There is no need to rush into losing your money. Wise players bide their time, and look, listen and learn. Wait until you feel confident in your poker skills before you play for money. And remember, never play with money that you cannot afford to lose

We will concentrate in the main on the way *No limit Texas Hold 'em* is played in poker tournaments. This is the form with which you are most likely to be familiar if you have watched poker on TV, and so is a good place to start.

1. Each player is dealt two cards face down. The *deal* rotates around the table, with the dealer being indicated by a *buck* or *button.*
2. The first player to the left of the button bets $1. This is the mandatory *small blind.*
3. The second player is called the *big blind* and bets $2.
4. Betting then proceeds around the table. A round of betting is never complete until everybody in the pot has put in the same amount of money, or passed.
5. If a player *raises,* the next player to act has three options: (a) to *pass,* which is to throw your hand in; (b) to *call,* that is put the same sum in the pot as the raiser; (c) himself to raise, and wager more than the previous bettor.
6. The action passes round the table and each player who has yet to act must at least match the money wagered by the previous person still in the pot.
7. Eventually it comes to the button, or dealer. When he has acted, the small blind must act. He may pass, call or raise. If nobody has raised, he must at least call $1, or pass.

8. If nobody has raised when it reaches the big blind, he may either *check*, which is to take no betting action at this stage, or raise. If he checks, then everybody has put the same amount of money into the middle.

9. Any player who, when it comes to his turn, has yet to match the money of the last raiser, has the right himself to raise.

10. Once everybody has wagered the same amount in any poker game, we move to the next stage.

11. In the case of Texas Hold 'em, the *flop* is dealt. First the top card is discarded unseen or *burnt*. Then three communal cards are dealt face up in the middle.

12. Betting then proceeds from the first person after the button due to act. He may check or bet. As it goes around the table, each player has the option. Once somebody has raised, the next person to act has the option of passing, calling or raising.

13. Once the money has been equalized we proceed to the next stage.

14. This is called *the turn*. Again a card is burnt and a fourth communal card is dealt face up.

15. There is another betting interval.

16. After the money is equalized, a third card is burnt and a fifth and final communal card is dealt face up. This is called *the river*.

17. After the final betting interval, the cards are shown and the best hand wins the pot.

18. Each player may use none of his own cards, which is called *playing the board*, or one or two of his own *hole cards*, in addition to three or four of the five communal cards.

19. When there are several players in the hand and one has used all his money, he is said to be *all-in*. He can only win the money in the main pot. Betting continues between the players still in action who have chips or money.

Texas hold ’em

Texas Hold ’em, Omaha and Seven Card Stud are the most popular forms of poker. Here are the basic rules of Texas Hold ’em.

1. Each player is dealt two cards face down. There is one round of betting on these cards. The deal moves to the left after each hand.

2. The top card is discarded unseen, or burnt.

3. Three cards are now dealt face up and placed in the centre of the table (the flop). These are to be used by all players still in the hand. A second round of betting takes place.

4. Another card is burnt.

5. A fourth card is dealt face up (the turn or fourth street) and added to the flop, after which there is a further round of betting.

6. There is a final burn card, and a fifth and final face up card (the river or fifth street) is added to the flop. The last round of betting takes place.

7. Each player has two cards, and the use of the five flop cards. This means each player has seven cards in their hand.

8. The winning hand is that of the player with the best five cards from the seven available. A player may use one, two or neither of the original cards dealt to him. If none are used, this is called playing the board.

SAMPLE HAND 1

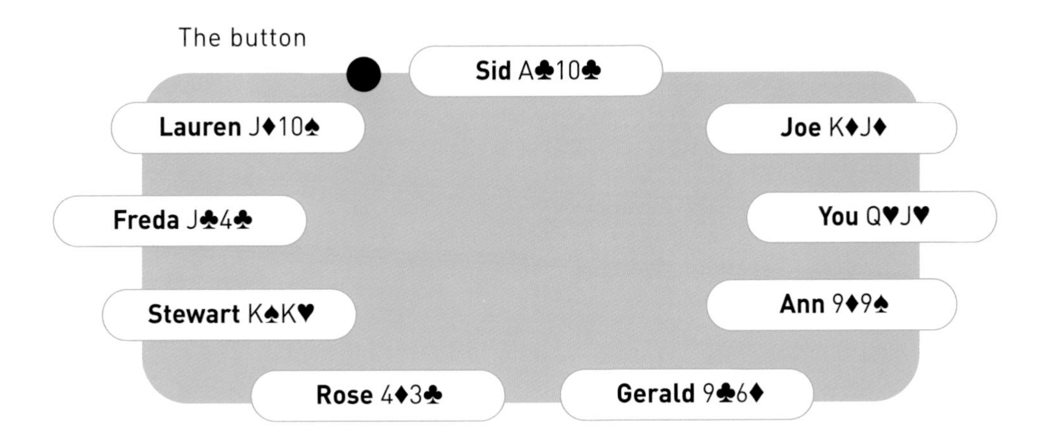

Lauren is the dealer, and so has the buck, or button, to her left. **Sid** is therefore first to bet, and bets the mandatory $1 (as the small blind). Joe is second, and so bets the mandatory $2 (as the big blind). **You** call. **Ann** calls. **Gerald** and **Rose** pass. The pot is $7. **Stewart** raises $20. **Freda** and **Lauren** pass. **Sid**, **Joe**, **You** and **Ann** all call. The pot is $110.

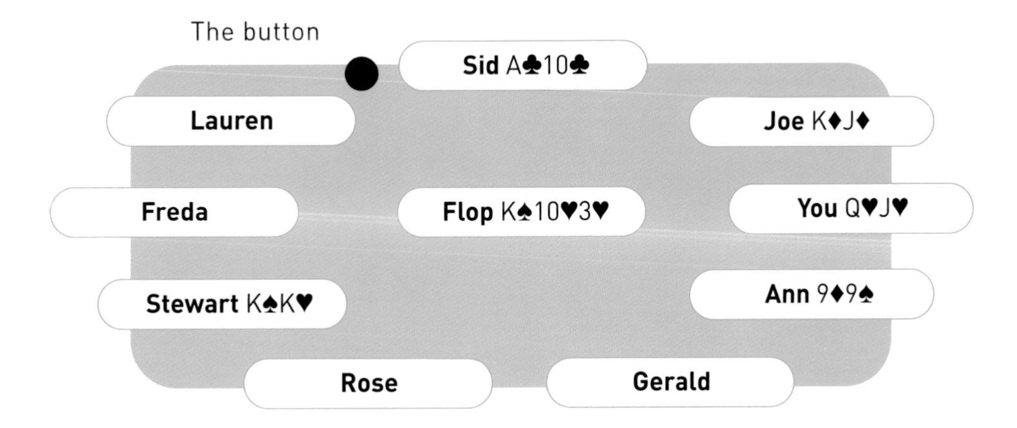

The Flop K♠10♥3♥

Sid checks. **Joe** bets $200. **You** call. **Ann** passes. **Stewart** raises $2000. **Sid** and **Joe** pass. **You** call. The pot is $4710.

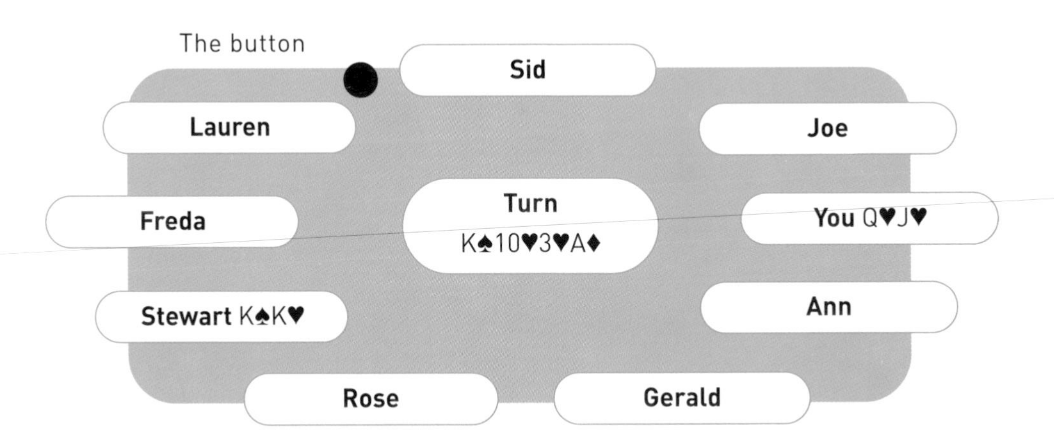

The Turn K♠10♥3♥A♦

You check. **Stewart** bets $10,000. **You** raise $50,000. Stewart calls. The pot is $124,710.

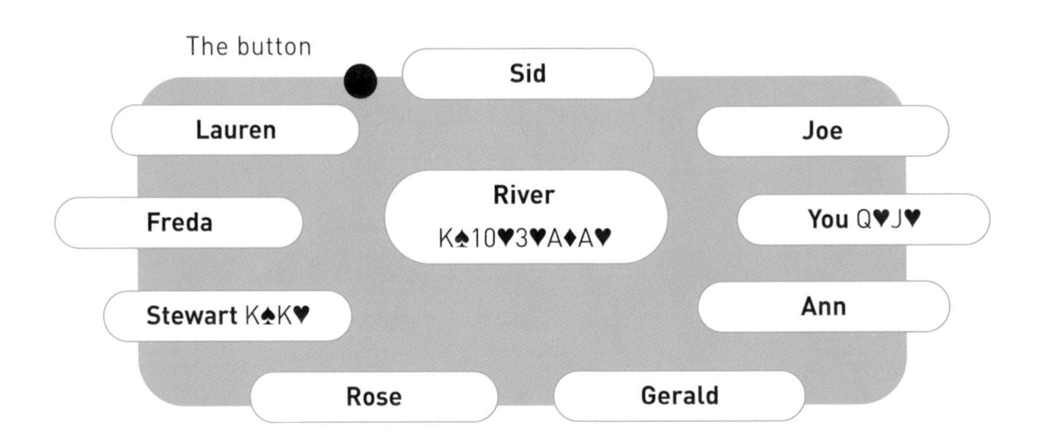

The River K♠10♥3♥A♦A♥

You check. **Stewart** bets $100,000, which is all the chips you have left. **You** call. The pot is $324,710.

Your best hand is 10♥3♥A♥Q♥J♥ a flush.

Stewart's best hand is K♠A♦A♥K♠K♥ a full house.

Stewart wins—well I did write the book.

ANALYSIS OF HAND 1

Generally you should not play in a pot in the early stages of a tournament with a hand weaker than two cards of Ten or better, or a pair, or possibly an Ace with a small card of the same suit. Thus **Rose** and **Gerald** did the correct thing. They passed.

I held a pair of Kings. This is the second-best hand in Texas Hold 'em before the flop. I should raise. Freda passed. Had there been no raise, it would be OK for **Lauren** to call with J♦10♠. **Sid, Joe, You** and **Ann** all called. It is unusual for there to be as many as five players in a Texas hold 'em hand.

Sid made a pair of Tens on the flop. It is highly likely that somebody has a King with so many players in the hand. He did well to check. **Joe** made a pair of Kings with a Jack *kicker*. Betting is reasonable. **You** have made an exceptionally strong drawing hand, four to an up-and-down straight and a flush draw. You have 15 cards with which to make one of those two hands. You are favorite to improve by the river. **You** decide to call, but could well have raised.

Of course **I** raised with *trip* Kings, which is the *nuts*. **Sid** passed as did **Joe**. He recognized trouble ahead. Many players would call, but remember: all anybody needs is a KQ to be beating him. **You** called. Again **You** might very well have reraised.

On the Turn **You** have made the nuts with an Ace high straight. Sneakily **You** check. **I** fall headlong into your trap and bet. Of course **I** had no way of knowing **You** had a straight. It was much more likely **You** had a flush draw.

Now **You** raised. I can win $74,710 for $50,000. My odds are 74,710/50,000 = about 3/2. I have seen six cards, which leaves 46 unseen. That leaves 46 of which 10 make me a full house or four of a kind. The odds against making the hand are (46-10)/10 = 3.6/1. I should pass, unless I think **You** are *bluffing*, or raising with an inferior hand. In that case I should raise the rest of the money. Of course, being the author, **I** had taken a peep at the last card.

On the river an open pair appeared. Your hand had "improved" from a straight to a

flush. **You** checked and **I** bet the last of your money (called *setting you in*). Understandably you called $100,000.

Note: It would never be allowed to bet more money than you have left. You can never be forced out of a poker hand just because you have insufficient funds. I have never, ever played in a poker game where there was this much money at stake. Poker can be played perfectly happily with a $5 *buy-in*. The strategy is the same whether it is $5 or $50,000, provided you can afford to lose. Never, ever play with money you cannot afford to lose. Usually in No Limit Texas Hold 'em there is simply a bet and a raise, then one player runs out of money.

Starting hands at Texas Hold 'em

When constructing a building, if you start with shaky foundations, then your whole edifice is likely to crumble. Thus it is in Texas Hold 'em. It is true that it is possible to hit any hand in this game, depending on the flop. But the fact of the matter is the best starting hand is likely to end up as the best hand after all the cards are out. Thus a pair of Aces is the best possible hand before the flop. AA is 9/2 favorite over KK if all the money goes in before the flop.

But pairs are not the only type of hand with which to win a hand. You may make a *straight* or *flush*. Let us consider some different starting hands which can lead to straights, using three cards from the board.

Holding	Straights	Number straights	Number nut straights
A-K	Q-J-10	1	1
K-Q	A-J-10, J-10-9	2	2
Q-J	A-K-10, K-10-9, 10-9-8	3	3
J-10	A-K-Q, K-Q-9, Q-9-8, 9-8-7	4	4
10-9	K-Q-J, Q-J-8, J-8-7, 8-7-6	4	3
10-8	Q-J-9, J-9-7, 9-7-6	3	2
10-7	J-9-8, 9-8-6	2	1
10-6	9-8-7	1	0

In order to make four possible straights, the two cards must be running, called *connectors*. For all your straights to be the nuts, your two cards must be 10 or above.

If your two cards are of the same suit, then it is more likely you will make a flush. Obviously the higher your first card, the more likely it is that your flush will be winning. Thus, from this viewpoint, A♥6♥ is much better than 9♥8♥. However with the former hand you will need **four** cards to make a straight. K-Q-J-10, 5-4-3-2, 10-9-8-7, 9-8-7-5, 8-7-5-4, 7-5-4-3 or 5-4-3-2 will be needed. This is much less likely and, moreover, only two of those combinations are the nuts.

If you are up against A♥A♣ then the best hand you can have before the flop is A♠A♦. Failing that, such as 8♠7♠ is your best chance. But 10♠9♠ would be utterly dominant if up against that holding.

Battle-ground before the flop

Hand	Objective	Disguise
A♣A♠	To get as much money in as possible	Not to make it clear you have Aces
K♦K♥	To get as much money in as possible, unless playing against Aces	Not to make it clear you have a high pair
A♠K♦	To build a big pot against weaker hands	Not to make it clear you have high cards
Q♦Q♣	To build a pot against weaker hands, but not to risk everything against AK	Not to make it clear you have a high pair
7♦7♣	To reach the flop cheaply or to push everybody out	For nobody to have any idea of your hand
7♦6♦	To reach the flop cheaply	To represent high cards

Of course in No Limit Texas Hold 'em, the money is often all-in before the flop. Then disguise counts for nothing. But don't be deceived by what you see on TV. They almost always only show the later stages of a tournament. Most hands are then just a bet and

raise. When playing for money or at the early stages of a tournament, there may be betting and raising at every stage.

The three ways of betting in Texas Hold 'em

No Limit You may bet or raise any amount you like at any stage until you run out of money. If there are more than two players left, you must raise more than the previous bettor, unless you run out of money.

Pot Limit At any stage you may only bet, or raise, up to the size of the pot after you have called. You do not have to raise the full size. You must raise more than the previous bet, if there are more than two players left, unless you run out of money.

Limit You can only bet or raise a certain pre-specified amount, which is independent of the amount in the pot and is often much smaller than the pot. If there are more than two players in the pot, only three raises are allowed.

The strategy and the value of the hands before the flop depend on which type of game you are playing. Also the strategy varies depending on whether you are playing in a cash game or a *tournament* and also the stage of the tournament. It is best to be on the button. In Texas Hold 'em, the later you are to speak, the better are your chances of winning money. In all forms of poker, *position* is especially valuable if you have a *drawing* hand rather than a *made hand.*

Nearly 30 years ago Dave Sklansky wrote an excellent book, *Hold 'em Poker*. This provides a list of the order of merit of the Texas Hold 'em hands before the flop. The following list is similar to that one, but it is provided for all types of poker. In No Limit, the value of the made hands, such as pairs, goes up. In Limit poker, the value of the drawing cards, such as suited connectors, goes up.

Hand	Group	**Hand**	Group	**Hand**	Group	**Hand**	Group	**Hand**	Group
A-A	1	Q-Js	5	6-6	6	J-9s	7	Q-8s	8
K-K	2	9-9	5	5-5	6	Q-9s	7	J-8s	8
Q-Q	2	A-J	5	4-4	6	Q-10	7	5-3s	8
A-Ks	2	J-10s	5	3-3	6	K-10	7	K-Xs	8
A-K	2	K-10s	5	2-2	6	10-9	7	J-9	9
A-Qs	3	8-8	5	9-8s	6	9-8	7	Q-9	9
A-Js	3	K-J	5	8-7s	6	8-7	7	K-9	9
J-J	3	Q-J	5	7-6s	6	7-6	7	Q-8s	9
K-Qs	3	10-9s	5	6-5s	6	6-5	7	J-7s	9
A-Q	3	A-10	6	5-4s	6	5-4	7	9-7s	9
A-10s	4	Q-10s	6	K-9s	7	A-X	7	8-6s	9
10-10	4	7-7	6	J-10	7	10-8s	8	7-5s	9
K-Q	4	6-6	6	10-9	7	J-7s	8	6-4s	9
A-Xs	4	5-5	6	9-8	7	9-7s	8	4-3s	9
K-Js	4	4-4	6	8-7	7	8-6s	8	5-3s	9

s is used to denote two cards of the same suit.

X stands for a card of undefined denomination.

Hands in the same group can all be played in much the same way.

It bears reiterating that this is the order of **playing** merit of the hands. J-3 is better all-in against 10-9, but it is a worthless load of garbage in any other situation, especially against several opponents. Heads-up, Q-7 is approximately even money all-in against an opponent who holds two random hole cards. So what?

Of course, there are many more hands than the 75 listed above. In a way it would be boring to list them. I was talking to young, very young, players recently. It became clear they thought K-7 was some type of hand. It doesn't even make it to the list multi-handed.

A pair of Nines is a watershed hand. It is approximately even money to be the best hand on the table against eight opponents who have yet to act. Thus, immediately somebody raises in a nine-handed game, you should move your requirements up to Group 4. You will only reraise with a Group 3 hand in Pot Limit or No Limit.

There is a great deal to be said for never calling the blind, only to pass or raise. This may be even more true of limit poker than pot limit or no limit.

In the early stages of a tournament, you don't want to fritter away your money calling with mediocre hands, only to have to pass when somebody raises. You should only call in late position, where you are less likely to be raised, or with the intention of reraising if another player takes action.

When drawing before the flop, you want to risk less than 5% of the money you have on the table.

No Limit Texas Hold 'em

SAMPLE HAND 2

Sid is in the small blind and thus bets $1. He holds Q♥4♦. **Joe** is in the big blind $2 with 9♠7♦. **You** hold J♦J♣ and have $1000 on the table. **You** make it $20 to play. **Ann** has Q♣9♣ and passes. **Gerald** has A♣5♠ and passes. **Rose** has 8♠7♠ and calls. The pot is $43. **Stewart** holds 5♥5♦ and calls. **Freda** holds Q♦8♣ and passes. **Lauren** has K♠3♦ and passes as do **Sid** and **Joe**.

The flop 10♦5♠2♣. The pot stands at $63. **You** hold J♦J♣, **Rose** has 8♠7♠. **I** hold 5♥5♦. **You** bet $100. **Rose** passes and **I** call.

The turn 10♦5♠2♣J♥. The pot stands at $263. **You** hold J♦J♣, **I** hold 5♥5♦. **You** bet $400. The pot is $663 and **I** raise $480 all-in. **You** call.

The river 10♦5♠2♣J♥6♥. **You** hold J♦J♣, **I** hold 5♥5♦. **You** win a pot of $2023 against **me**.

ANALYSIS OF HAND 2

Your pair of Jacks is a pretty good hand. You never have to raise, but this is as good a time as any. Sometimes you can get yourself into **more** trouble by not raising. If you call and another player raises, you do not know whether it is because he is strong or because he thinks you are weak.

In poker aggression is usually the best policy.

Any two cards above a Five is very nearly even money against a pair of Fives. Any higher pair is a big, big favorite.

Rose called with suited connectors in late position. That is fine. She can win another $1000 and is risking $20.

I called with a pair of Fives. Of course, it is entirely possible that this hand is currently winning. But the fact is you do not want to get involved with low pairs.

In poker, or in life, try to avoid situations where you are either a small favorite or a big underdog.

So why call at all? It is basically to hit trip Fives on the flop. This is 7/1 against. The pot is $43 and it is $20 to me. Clearly the odds are not there. **I** am calling, as did **Rose,** in the hope of making a big hand and making a killing. **I** am in a better position than she is. Should it come a *blank* for either of us, **You** will bet and we will kiss our $20 goodbye.

Came the flop and **You** bet. That is perfectly reasonable—you are probably winning. **Rose** passes, her hand being worthless. **I** have hit the trip Fives. This is my *ticket to the river*. I can't worry about trip Tens in Texas Hold 'em. **I** can either call or raise. If **I** raise and **You** have nothing, that will be the end of the pot. But what if you have AK and either card comes on the turn? Then I may get paid off. A call seems in order because I have position on you.

Came the turn and **You** have made a monster of a hand. Many people will check in this position for fear of frightening away the opposition. This is not the way to get rich. Thus

You come out betting $400. Of course, **I** raised all-in; of course **You** called and of course **You** won a nice pot.

Did you think I was going to win again by hitting *quad* Fives? Ha, got you! I bluffed you within the confines of a book. In real life such dramatic events as this pot or the previous one are very rare. So far I have chosen extreme examples in order to help you familiarize yourself with the grammar of poker.

SAMPLE HAND 3

So far we have played Texas Hold 'em with open cards, just like on TV. Now you are going to play and have to make decisions. Each hand will be a quiz. Sadly I am not awarding prizes for the correct answers, but hopefully your opponents will, when you come to play for money.

The blinds are $1 $2. Seats 3 and 4 have passed and **Sid** has *limped in* for $2. Seat 6 passes and **You** are in seat 7 with A♥J♥.

Question 1: Should **You** (a) pass (b) call (c) raise $2 (d) raise $10 (e) raise $100?
Answer 1: (a) 0 (b) 5 (c) 2 (d) 10 (e) 0
Reason 1: Your hand is in Group 3 and you have good position. Raising $2 *shops the business* that you like your hand, but is not enough money to drive anybody out. If you raise $100, everybody will probably pass. But occasionally you will come up against a monster and lose your money. You would be risking $102 to win $5.
Action 1: You raise $10 and only **Sid** calls.

The flop 9♠7♦4♣. The pot is $27. **You** hold A♥J♥.

Sid checks.

Question 2: Should **You** (a) check (b) bet $10 (c) bet $30 (d) bet $40 (e) bet $100?
Answer 2: (a) 0 (b) 4 (c) 10 (d) 10 (e) 0
Reason 2: You are probably winning and don't want to give a free card. Betting too little or too much could be dangerous.

Action 2: You bet $30 and **Sid** passes.
This is a standard coup that you will see played every day. Usually nobody connects with the flop.

Score:	
20	Well done, but it wasn't rocket science.
10-15	You were not aggressive enough.
4-9	This is No Limit and you aren't betting enough.
0-3	Start again from the beginning.

SAMPLE HAND 4
The blinds are $1 $2. It is a No Limit tournament and you have $1000 in chips, somewhat above average. **Sid** and **Joe** pass. **You** hold 9♦8♦.

Question 1: Should **You** (a) pass (b) call $2 (c) raise $2 (d) raise $10 (e) raise $100?
Answer 1: (a) 10 (b) 5 (c) 2 (d) 4 (e) 0
Reason 1: You are in mid-position and have a mediocre hand, why not be patient?

Don't limp in except in late position, especially in a tournament.

Action 1: You call. **Ann** raises $10, **Rose** calls and everybody else passes. **Ann** has $400 in chips and **Rose** $1000.

The pot stands at $29. It is $10 to you.

Question 2: Should **You** (a) pass (b) call (c) raise $10 (d) raise $50 (e) raise $200?
Answer 2: (a) 10 (b) 6 (c) 0 (d) 2 (e) 1
Reason 2: Naturally other people would score this differently. You have given yourself a minor headache by calling loosely in mid-position.
Action 2: You call.

The flop Q♦8♠2♥. The pot is $39. **You** hold 9♦8♦.

Question 3: Should **You** (a) check (b) bet $25 (c) bet $50 (d) bet $100 (e) bet $400 (f) bet $1000?
Answer 3: (a) 10 (b) 4 (c) 10 (d) 2 (e) 0 (f) 0
Reason 3: You have second best pair. You may or may not be winning. Problems, problems, all caused by your poor position. You could set **Ann** in, but it is a big proportion of your *stack* to risk if called by either player.
Action 3: You check. **Ann** bets $60, she has $340 left and **Rose** passes.

The flop Q♦8♠2♥. The pot is $99. **You** hold 9♦8♦ and the bet is $60.

Question 4: Should **You** (a) pass (b) call (c) raise $60 (d) raise $200 (e) raise $340 all-in?
Answer 4: (a) 6 (b) 8 (c) 2 (d) 8 (e) 10
Reason 4: Mostly in Texas Hold 'em this is about the best you can expect to happen. Life is not about flopping trips, two pair, made straights or flushes. Your decision will partly be based on how **Ann** plays. If you do raise, one thing is favorable. You are attacking the *short stack* and, if you lose the hand, you will not be mortally wounded.

In a tournament, always try to attack the short stacks.

Raising $60 to see how the land lies is a fruitless exercise. Be a man!

Don't send a boy on a man's errand.

Action 4: You raise $340 all-in and **Ann** passes. You have risked $412 and won $87. If the flop had been K♦8♠2♥, that play would have been much more risky. It is quite likely **Ann** has a King, and she won't pass a raise. If the worst comes to the worst and **Ann** calls, she probably has such as AQ. You can still win with a Nine or Eight. That is about 4/1 against and you are going to find yourself in worse situations than that if you are going to play poker properly.

Don't worry when you come up against a *brick wall*. This happens all the time in poker and, provided you played correctly, you should have no regrets.

Score:

40	Had Ann doubled-up, would you be feeling so smug?
30-39	The decisions are difficult with such a marginal hand.
20-29	Well, you haven't been playing poker very long.
10-19	Reread the chapter.
0-9	You haven't got the hang of things yet.

Pot Limit Texas Hold 'em

In this game, the maximum you can bet or raise at any stage is the size of the pot. The purpose here was to make the game even simpler. It is a very good idea to keep a running tally of the size of the pot in this game. Then you can *under-bet* the pot if you wish. Also you will know what odds you are getting.

When facing one bet, you can never have less than 2/1 for your money. Thus, unlike No Limit, it is more difficult to *kill the action.*

Now it will be easier to call with drawing hands such as 8♣7♣ or 6♦6♣ before the flop. But the difference from a cash No Limit Texas Hold 'em game is not enormous.

SAMPLE HAND 5

Here is our usual $1 $2 blinds game. **You** are first to speak after the blinds of **Sid** and **Joe**. The pot is $3 and **You** hold J♣9♣. There are the usual 6 suspects to act.

Question 1: Should **You** (a) pass (b) call (c) raise $2 (d) raise $5, the maximum?
Answer 1: (a) 10 (b) 4 (c) 2 (d) 5
Reason 1: Do you hear, "It's only $2," whispering in your ear? That is very seductive, but buildings built on shifting sands are only too likely to crumble. In a tournament the play would be even worse.
Action 1: You call. Everybody passes to **Stewart** and **I** raise $5, less than the maximum. **Lauren** calls $7 and **Joe** in the big blind calls $5.

The pot is $24 and it is $5 to **You** holding J♣9♣.

Question 2: Should **You** (a) pass (b) call $5 (c) raise $5 (d) raise $10 (e) raise $29?
Answer 2: (a) 0 (b) 10 (c) 0 (d) 0 (e) 2
Reason 2: You are getting nearly 5/1 for your money. These odds are too good to pass with almost any hand. At least you cannot be raised. Raising yourself would be crazy—but, if you must, a full-blooded raise is required, not a baby one.
Action 2: You call.

The flop 9♥ 7♣ 2♣. **You** hold J♣9♣. **Joe** is first to speak and bets $25. The pot is $54.

Question 3: Should **You** (a) pass (b) call (c) raise $25 (d) raise $99?
Answer 3: (a) 0 (b) 10 (b) 5 (d) 8
Reason 3: This is an example of *Morton's Fork*. Either you are winning against **Joe** or **You** have the only flush draw. It would be insane to pass.
Action 3: You call. **Stewart** raises $100 and **Joe** calls. The pot is $329 and it is $100 to you. You have $450 left.

Question 4: Should you (a) pass (b) call (c) raise $100 (d) raise $350 all-in?
Answer 4: (a) 10 (b) 8 (c) 0 (d) 8
Reason 4: You have been *whip-lashed*. That means you've been bet at from your right-hand side and then raised from the left. The most likely answer is that one opponent has you beaten and the other a better flush draw. But surely you have good pot odds and can anyway hit two pair or trips? Anybody would find this difficult to pass. Raising in the hope of dislodging the better draw can certainly be considered. You are likely to go all-in anyway, if you call.
Action 4: You call.

The turn 9♥ 7♣ 2♣8♦. **You** hold J♣9♣. The pot is $429 and you have $350 left. The others have about $1500. **Joe** checks.

Question 5: Should **You** (a) check (b) bet $100 (c) bet $350 all-in?
Answer 5: (a) 10 (b) 0 (c) 4

Reason 5: You really want a free card - and may get one. **You** could do worse than going all-in. If you can reduce it to one opponent you have a very fair shot at the pot. **You** can even make a straight with a Ten. If **You** bet and **Stewart** raises, **Joe** may wilt under the pressure.
Action 5: You check, **Stewart** bets $250 and **Joe** calls. The pot is $929.

Question 6: Should **You** (a) pass (b) call $250 (c) raise $100 all-in?
Answer 6: (a) 10 (b) 8 (c) -2
Reason 6: Why does **Stewart** keep betting substantially less than the pot? **You** are getting nearly 4/1 for your money. This is difficult to resist. Raising $100 all-in would be crazy. Neither opponent will pass and surely you are beaten in at least one spot.
Action 6: You call.

The river 9♥ 7♣ 2♣8♦K♦. **You** hold J♣9♣. **Joe** checks. The pot is $1179. You have $100.

Question 7: Should **You** (a) check (b) bet $100 all-in?
Answer 7: (a) 10 (b) 0
Reason 7: Why waste $100?
Action 7: You check. **Stewart** checks. He has Q♥Q♣ and **Joe** has A♣10♣.
Stewart recognized the danger of **Joe** having A♣K♣ and simply checked the hand down. Had he bet the river, would **You** have been able to resist calling for $100?

Score:	
70	Terrific, don't apply to play in my game.
60-69	An excellent score.
50-59	Still highly acceptable.
40-49	Remember those school reports, could do better?
30-39	This is just not good enough.
20-29	Perhaps it would all have come out better in real life.
10-19	Read it all again.
-2 to 9	Do not yet play poker for money—except against me.

SAMPLE HAND 6

Stewart is on the small blind for $1 and **Freda** the big blind for $2. **Lauren** and **Sid** pass, while **Joe** calls. **You** hold A♦K♦. The pot is $5.

Question 1: Should **You** (a) pass (b) call $2 (c) raise $2 (d) raise $7, making it $9 to go?
Answer 1: (a) 0 (b) 2 (c) 2 (d) 10
Reason 1: You have a *premium hand* and only **Joe** has so far shown interest.
Action 1: You make it $9. **Ann** and **Gerald** pass. **Rose** reraises $23, **Stewart** calls and **Freda** passes. **Joe** calls. The pot is $107 and it is $23 to **You**. **You** hold A♦K♦.

Question 2: Should **You** (a) pass (b) call (c) raise $23 (d) raise $50 (e) raise $130?
Answer 2: (a) 8 (b) 10 (c) 7 (d) 2 (e) 4
Reason 2: Your hand was very strong, but now, not only has **Rose** raised, but **Stewart** and **Joe** have called a double raise. Head-up **You** are not favorite against any pair. You are entitled to be worried that you are up against Aces or Kings. The advantage of A♦K♦ is that it is not inferior to any pair of Queens or below and both of the dreaded best pairs are unlikely. That advantage has evaporated. **Rose** even has position on **You**.
Action 2: You call.

The flop Q♦8♦2♣. **You** hold A♦K♦. The pot is $130. **Stewart** and **Joe** check. Each player has $1000 left.

Question 3: Should **You** (a) check (b) bet $30 (c) bet $60 (d) bet $100 (e) bet $130?
Answer 3: (a) 10 (b) 2 (c) 4 (d) 10 (e) 10
Reason 3: You have a premium flush draw, but the possibility of hitting an Ace or King is not as attractive as usual. It is likely **Rose** will bet. Why not let her get on with it and see the reaction of the other players?
Action 3: You check. **Rose** bets $130 and **Joe** calls. The pot is $390 and it is $130 to **You**.

Question 4: Should **You** (a) pass (b) call (c) raise $130 (d) raise $500?
Answer 4: (a) 4 (b) 10 (c) 0 (d) 5

Reason 4: You are only 2/1 against making the flush by the river and getting 3/1 for your money. **BUT** it is likely there will be a bet on the turn, meaning you will have to put more money in to the pot.

Money odds on the flop are illusory. There will probably be further betting on the turn.

If **You** could be certain either both players will pass or both call, if you raise, then it is worthwhile to be super-aggressive. Raise $500 and be willing to go all-in.

Action 4: You call.

The turn Q♦8♦2♣7♥. **You** hold A♦K♦. The pot is $520 and all three players have $870 left. **Joe** checks.

Question 5: Should **You** (a) check (b) bet $100 (c) bet $250 (d) bet $500?
Answer 5: (a) 10 (b) 1 (c) 0 (d) 0
Reason 5: There is no reason for heroics. To reopen the betting for **Joe** by betting $100 seems just plain daft.
Action 5: You check. **Rose** bets $500 and **Joe** calls. The pot is $1520 and it is $500 to **You**. There is $370 left to bet, should **You** call.

Question 6: Should **You** (a) pass (b) call (c) raise $370 all-in?
Answer 6: (a) 10 (b) 4 (c) 0
Reason 6: You can see 6 cards. Thus **You** cannot see 46. There are 9 diamonds unaccounted for. (46-9)/9 makes it approximately 4/1 against your making the flush. You are only getting a little better than 3/1 for your money. Let us assume that **You** hit your flush, bet $370 and are called. Then **You** will win $1520 + $370 = $1890.

The Implied Odds is an important factor in poker when deciding whether to call. But you need a great deal of money for this to come into consideration on the river.

$1890/$500 = 3.8/1. This is the *Implied Odds.* The money you will win if you hit your hand. It is still not quite good enough. There is another factor. If either of your opponents has trips, **You** would have only 7 winning diamonds. That should be enough to clinch it for you.

Action 6: You pass and we lose interest in the hand. You want to know how it came out? The river Q♦8♦2♣7♥5♣. **Joe** checked, **Rose** bet and **Joe** passed. Their cards will remain an eternal mystery. I haven't thought of it before, but this would be one advantage of playing on TV. You would eventually find out what cards players had.

Score:	
60	If you keep making these scores, you have already graduated.
50-59	An excellent score.
40-49	Not at all bad.
30-39	You probably need to understand odds better.
20-29	You definitely need to understand odds better.
10-19	Are you remembering to take into account the cards of the other players?
0-9	This is very disappointing.

Limit raise Texas Hold 'em

- Similar to the game described in detail on pages 144 and 145, but the betting system differs considerably. The small blind bets $1 and the big blind $2 as before. Then each player may pass, call or raise.
- However the maximum raise before the flop is $2. While there are more than two players in the hand, the maximum number of raises at any stage is three.*
- When all the betting is done and the players have wagered the same amount, the flop is dealt.
- Then the first player may check or bet. His bet must be $2, no more, no less.
- Again when the bets are equalized, the turn card is dealt.
- Again there is a betting interval. But this time the bet must be $4.
- Again when the betting round is finished, the river card is dealt.
- There is a final betting interval where again the maximum bet or raise is $4.

* *Some poker sites on the Internet permit only three raises, even if there are only two players.*

SAMPLE HAND 7

Freda is in the small blind with $1. **Lauren** is in the big blind with $2. **Sid** passes and **Joe** makes it $4 to go. **You** hold A♣J♠. There is $7 in the pot.

Question 1: Should **You** (a) pass (b) call (c) raise $2?
Answer 1: (a) 0 (b) 10 (c) 8
Reason 1: This is a moderately good hand. By raising you would be discouraging *tourists* from competing. You have only one more raise to fear. This idea of putting pressure on other players with a double raise is a common one, even though you know your opponent may stand better. Even so, your hand is not that great, it ranks under a pair of Nines.
Action 1: You call. **Ann** and **Gerald** call. All pass to **Lauren** who is in the big blind. **She** raises. **Joe** calls. There is $25 in the pot. **You** hold A♣J♠.

Question 2: Should **You** (a) pass (b) call (c) raise $2?
Answer 2: (a) -2 (b) 10 (c) 2
Reason 2: It is far too late to pass now. Your odds are far too great. A raise would be a futile gesture, nobody is going out.
Action 2: You, Ann and **Gerald** all call.

The flop K♦J♣6♣. **You** hold A♣J♠. The pot is $31.

Lauren bets $2. **Joe** passes. The pot is $33. **Ann** and **Gerald** have yet to act.

Question 3: Should **You** (a) pass (b) call (c) raise $2?
Answer 3: (a) 2 (b) 8 (c) 10
Reason 3: You are probably losing, but at least have a pair of Jacks. If **You** hit a Jack or Ace you will probably be winning. By raising you are putting real pressure on **Ann** and **Gerald**. It will cost each of them $4 to call and they are facing a possible extra $4. There is something else, **You** hold the A♣. Neither of them has the nut flush. You do not want them fishing around in the pot.

Yet another thing. **You** are raising $2. **Lauren** may not reraise. Indeed she may not bet the turn. Then **You** will reach the river at a cost of only $2.

Action 3: You raise $2; **Ann** and **Gerald** pass. **Lauren** just calls.

The turn K♦J♣6♣2♥. **You** hold A♣J♠. **Lauren** checks. The pot is $39.

Question 4: Should **You** (a) check (b) bet $4?
Answer 4: (a) 10 (b) 7
Reason 4: You can grab your chance of a free card, or are **You** giving **Lauren** a free card, or can **You** put her under pressure and get her to pass?
Action 4: You check.

The river K♦J♣6♣2♥8♦. **You** hold A♣J♠.

Lauren checks. The pot is $39.

Question 5: Should **You** (a) check (b) bet $4?
Answer 5: (a) 10 (b) 3
Reason 5: If **You** bet, with what is **Lauren** going to call where **You** are winning?
Action 5: You check. **Lauren** turns over Q♥Q♦. She wins. Would she have wilted and passed had you bet the turn and river? Who can say? She might have read **You** for a flush draw and felt she had to call.

Gerald grumbles that he had passed the winning hand, K♥10♦. He continues to look daggers at **You** for some time. Eventually he gets involved in another pot with **You** and throws off some nice money in exasperation. Thus the investment of the $2 raise comes back in an unexpected way.

Score:	
50	Excellent. Perhaps I am a good teacher?
40-49	You have got a feel for this game extremely quickly.
30-39	Don't despair.
20-29	Perhaps limit Texas Hold 'em will click later.
10-19	A very disappointing score.
-2 to 9	Reread the material.

SAMPLE HAND 8

Ann is in the small blind for $1 and **Gerald** the big blind for $2. **Rose, Stewart** and **Lauren** call $2. **Sid** passes and **Joe** calls.

You are last to speak. **You** hold K♦8♠. The pot is $11.

Question 1: Should **You** (a) pass (b) call (c) raise $2?
Answer 1: (a) 10 (b) 2 (c) 0
Answer 1: It is true **You** have 11/2 odds, but your hand is filth. GIGO, garbage in garbage out, is just as true in poker as it is in computers.
Action 1: You call. **Ann** raises $2, **Gerald** passes and the other four players call. The pot is $24. It is $2 to **You** and **You** hold K♦8♠.

Question 2: Should **You** (a) pass (b) call $2 (c) raise $2?
Answer 2: (a) -2 (b) 10 (c) 1
Reason 2: You cannot pass up odds of 12/1. **You** have to grit your teeth and bear it.
Action 2: You call.

The flop K♠7♦2♦. **You** hold K♦8♠. The pot is $26.

Ann bets $2. **Rose** and **Stewart** are the only callers. There is $32 in the pot.

Question 3: Should **You** (a) pass (b) call (c) raise $2?
Answer 3: (a) 0 (b) 10 (c) 1
Reason 3: Of course it is most unlikely you are winning, but while there's life there's hope and you are getting 16/1 for your money. At least **You** cannot be raised.
Action 3: You call.

The turn K♠7♦2♦8♥. **You** hold K♦8♠. The pot is $34.
Ann bets $4. **Rose** calls and **Stewart** folds. There is $42 in the pot.

Question 4: Should **You** (a) pass (b) call (c) raise $4?
Answer 4: (a) -2 (b) 5 (c) 10

Reason 4: You have probably stumbled into the best hand and must make the most of it.
Action 4: You raise $4 and **Ann** reraises $4. **Rose** calls. The pot is $58. **You** hold K♦8♠.

Question 5: Should **You** (a) pass (b) call (c) raise $4, the final raise?
Answer 5: (a) 0 (b) 10 (c) 4
Reason 5: You may have caught a tiger by the tail and be up against trip Kings, with no win. Anyway, another $4 is not going to shake anybody off.
Action 5: You call.

The river K♠7♦2♦8♥A♣. **You** hold K♦8♠. The pot is $62.

Ann bets $4 and **Rose** passes. The pot is $66.

Question 6: Should **You** (a) pass (b) call (c) raise $4?
Answer 6: (a) -2 (b) 10 (c) 0
Reason 6: You must make a *crying call*. That is a call where you think you have a loser, but the odds are too good to resist.
Action 6: You call and **Ann** shows down A♥K. You have been outdrawn on the river. **You** whinge a bit at the unfairness of it all. The truth is **You** played perfectly after the first call and lost $22. The error lay with that first *loose call*.

Score:

60	Is this your usual score?
50-59	Very well done.
40-49	Presumably you were sucked into the maelstrom of pot odds.
30-39	You would have to be much more careful in real life.
20-29	You may be at the bottom of the class.
10-19	This is dreadful.
-4 to 9	And this is even worse.

Limit games are often bigger than No Limit or Pot Limit. It depends on the structure. A $200—$400 limit game is bigger than any game in which I have played.

The game is played much faster than the other forms. There is much more action and you can rapidly come unstuck. It is a less pure form of poker because there is less bluffing, but it is a perfectly good money game and many prefer it. You can only bluff a really good player in Limit.

SAMPLE HAND 9

You are in the small blind for $1 and **Ann** in the big blind for $2. **Gerald** and **Rose** pass. **Stewart** raises $2. **Freda** calls and **Lauren** passes.

You hold K♦Q♦. The pot is $7 and it is $3 to **You**.

Question 1: Should **You** (a) pass (b) call (c) raise $2?
Answer 1: (a) 0 (b) 10 (c) 2
Reason 1: This is a Group 3 hand. There are those, I suppose, who would say you should pass virtually every hand when in the small blind. Personally I wouldn't have that much patience. Out of position though, it doesn't seem sensible to make the pot even bigger.
Action 1: You call as does **Ann.**

The flop 10♦9♣4♥. **You** hold K♦Q♦. The pot is $12.

Question 2: Should **You** (a) check (b) bet $2?
Answer 2: (a) 10 (b) 2
Reason 2: You only have a mediocre hand and would prefer a free card, or as cheap a one as possible.
Action 2: You check as does **Ann**. **Stewart** bets $2, **Freda** passes. The pot is $14.

Question 3: Should **You** (a) pass (b) call $2 (c) raise $2?
Answer 3: (a) 7 (b) 10 (c) 1
Reason 3: You have 7/1 for your money. **You** have four Jacks with which to hit a *middle-pin* straight. That is 11/1 against on the turn. But you may hit the winning hand with a King or Queen. Also **You** have good *implied odds.*

Do not fall into the trap of thinking it is only about 5/1 against hitting the straight by the river and the odds being offered are 7/1. There will probably be a bet on the turn and thus it will cost you $6 to reach the river.

Action 3: You call and **Ann** raises $2. **Stewart** reraises. The pot is $24 and it is $4 to **You**. There is one raise left.

Question 4: Should **You** (a) pass (b) call $4?
Answer 4: (a) 10 (b) 4
Reason 4: Now **You** are only getting 6/1 for your money and it is certain there will be a bet on the turn. On the other hand, here are two players gunning for **You** and this improves your implied odds. The trouble is, **Ann** may put in the final raise.
Action 4: You call as does **Ann**. Phew! The merry-go-round was getting a lot less merry.

The turn 10♦9♣4♥5♠. **You** hold K♦Q♦. The pot is $30.

Question 5: Should **You** (a) check (b) bet $4?
Answer 5: (a) 10 (b) 0
Reason 5: Your hand has not improved and betting would just cost **You** money.
Action 5: You check as does **Ann. Stewart** bets $4. The pot is $34.

Question 6: Should **You** (a) pass (b) call (c) raise $4?
Answer 6: (a) 10 (b) 3 (c) -2
Reason 6: Now **You** are getting 17/2 for your money. Also **Ann** is surely not going to pass, which makes it 19/2. **You** will certainly win more if **You** connect. **But** there is a real danger **Ann** intends to raise. **You** have no idea whether **You** will win if a King or Queen comes on the river, but it is likely not.
Action 6: You call. **Ann** raises and **Stewart** reraises. The pot is $54 and it is $8 to call. There is still one raise left for Ann if she wishes.

Question 7: Should **You** (a) pass (b) call?
Answer 7: (a) 10 (b) 2

Reason 7: There is no way you are going to win $88 in this hand. Even more than in No Limit or Pot Limit, you must respect the odds. Do **You** feel a little silly, having already called so many bets? Well, **You** should swallow your pride.
Action 7: **You** pass. **Ann** raises. **Stewart** called. I think readers will want to see what happened.

The river 10♦9♣4♥5♠6♣. **Ann** bets $4 and **Stewart** calls.

Ann wins with 10♥9♦ against **Stewart's** A♠10♠.

Did **I** overplay my hand? Arguably yes, but it could have been costly to allow **You** in cheaply.

Have you noticed how cleverly **Ann** played? By not putting in the third raise on the flop, she gave the impression her hand was not all that strong. She won more money and also forced **You** out.

Score:	
70	Extremely cautious and extremely good.
60-69	Excellent.
50-59	You should still become a winning player.
40-49	You need a great deal more work.
30-39	Reread the whole Texas Hold 'em chapter.
20-29	Don't play poker for money except against me.
10-19	Oh dear, oh dear.
-2 to 9	How did you manage that?

Limit poker is much more popular in the U.S. than in Europe. It is also frequently *spread* on the Internet. The game is played much faster than No Limit or Pot Limit. Since the swings are less dramatic, many professionals prefer this form of the game. But what they are really hungry for is weak players trying to lose their money.

If you aspire to be a professional, in order to maximize your opportunities, you should be versatile and play all games.

Omaha

Omaha is a game which flows naturally out of Texas Hold 'em. It's only been played since the 1980s.

- Each player receives four cards face down.
- The betting proceeds just like in Texas Hold 'em. (See pages 144 and 145.)
- The player **must** use **TWO** cards from his hand and **THREE** from the board.
- The game is always played either pot limit or limit.

Thus the game is essentially of **NINE** cards and this means it can become extremely complex.

You must first learn how to read the board so that this becomes second nature. Even then, I know of nobody who has not sometimes made a mistake—and that definitely includes me. So let us practice with the chart opposite.

As you can see, the possibilities are, at first glance, bewildering. However, a good Texas Hold 'em player like you should settle in soon enough. Practice will enable you to recognize the best hand on the flop, turn and river and also the best drawing hands on the flop and the turn. Unlike Texas Hold 'em, it is not unusual for the drawing hand to be better than the made one. Also often players have *matching cards*.

I recommend you spend some hours laying out flops and deciding which are the best possible hands and which the best drawing ones. Then repeat the exercise for the turn and the river. To be a winner, you want this to be your natural reaction at any time.

Each of the hands shows first the three flop cards, then the turn and finally the river. The first two are sheer fantasy. I have only once seen the second where one player had the nut full house, a second

The river	Player's cards	Player's two best	Hand held
A♥7♣5♥5♠A♠	A♦K♥Q♥J♦	A♦K♥	A♦A♥A♠K♥7♣
A♥7♣5♥5♠A♠	8♦7♥7♦6♦	7♥7♦	7♥7♦7♣5♥5
A♥7♣5♥5♠A♠	A♣10♦9♦7♠	A♣7♠	A♣A♥A♠7♠7♣
A♥7♣5♥5♠A♠	8♠6♣5♦5♣	5♦5♣	5♦5♣5♥5♠A♥
K♥10♦7♠J♦7♦	A♦Q♣J♥9♠	A♦Q♣	A♦K♥Q♣J♦10♦
K♥10♦7♠J♦7♦	K♣K♠Q♥9♣	K♣K♠	K♣K♠K♥7♠7♦
K♥10♦7♠J♦7♦	10♣10♠7♥7♣	7♥7♣	7♥7♣7♠7♦K♥
K♥10♦7♠J♦7♦	Q♠J♠9♦8♦	9♦8♦	J♦10♦9♦8♦7♦
Q♦J♦8♠7♦2♦	A♦J♠9♥2♣	J♠2♣	J♠J♦2♣2♦Q♦
Q♦J♦8♠7♦2♦	K♣Q♥10♠7♣	Q♥7♣	Q♥Q♦7♣7♦J♦
Q♦J♦8♠7♦2♦	A♥K♣7♥7♠	7♥7♠	7♥7♠7♦Q♦J♦
Q♦J♦8♠7♦2♦	J♥J♣4♦3♦	4♦3♦	4♦3♦Q♦J♦2♦
A♥A♦A♠A♣9♠	K♥Q♥J♦9♥	K♥Q♥	A♥A♦A♠K♥Q♥
A♥A♦A♠A♣9♠	Q♣J♦3♥3♦	3♥3♦	A♥A♦A♠3♥3♦
A♣10♦9♠6♣J♠	A♥Q♥9♦7♦	A♥9♦	A♥A♣9♦9♠J♠
A♣10♦9♠6♣J♠	10♥10♣5♥4♦	10♥10♣	10♥10♣10♦A♣J♠
A♣10♦9♠6♣J♠	A♠8♦7♠6♦	8♦7♠	J♠10♦9♠8♦7♠
A♣10♦9♠6♣J♠	K♥Q♠J♥8♣	K♥Q♠	A♣K♥Q♠J♥10♦

quads and the last a straight flush. The third is a more bread and butter hand, where the winner has a flush. I give the hand where the board is four of a kind because I have often seen players look completely bewildered when this has happened. The last shows a typical hand where a player has made a nut straight on the river.

The average winning hand at Omaha is roughly a straight.

The average winning hand at Texas Hold 'em is roughly two pair.

SAMPLE HAND 10

Stewart is in the small blind for $1 and **Freda** the big blind for $2. **Lauren a**nd **Sid** pass. **Joe** calls. The pot is $5 and it is $2 to **You**. It is pot limit. You hold 8♣7♦6♥4♣.

Question 1: Should **You** (a) pass (b) call (c) raise $2 (d) raise $7?

Answer 1: (a) -1 (b) 10 (c) 7 (d) 8

Reason 1: This is quite a strong hand at Omaha. You are looking for four cards that combine or a high pair. It isn't perfect: that would be 8♣7♦6♦5♣. The actual hand does not have *two* flush draws. A raise would be deceiving, because it inevitably suggests **You** have high cards. It is not to be recommended if you have an inveterate swashbuckler to follow.

Action 1: You call. **Ann** passes and **Gerald** raises $9. **Rose**, **Stewart** and **Joe** all call. There is $48 in the pot and it is $9 to **You** holding 8♣7♦6♥4♣.

Question 2: Should **You** (a) pass (b) call $9 (c) raise $9 (d) raise $25 (e) raise $57?

Answer 2: (a) -1 (b) 10 (c) 2 (d) 0 (e) 0

Reason 2: You have a drawing hand which cannot possibly be winning. What do **You** want players out of the pot for? **You** may hit absolutely nothing.

Action 2: You call. It is not unusual for there to be five players in the hand.

The flop A♣7♦6♥. **You** hold 8♣7♦6♥4♣. **Stewart** and **Joe** check. The pot is $57.

Question 3: Should **You** (a) check (b) bet $10 (c) bet $25 (d) bet $57?

Answer 3: (a) 10 (b) 0 (c) 0 (d) 4

Reason 3: You have hit quite a strong hand, two pair and a Five for a straight. **BUT** there is an Ace out there. **Gerald** may have trip Aces or Aces up. So might somebody else. Discretion is the better part of valor, a check is in order.

Action 3: You check. **Gerald** bets $50 and the other three all pass. The pot is $107 and it is $50 to **You**.

Question 4: Should **You** (a) pass (b) call (c) raise $50 (d) raise $157?

Answer 4: (a) 7 (b) 10 (c) 0 (d) 6

Reason 4: You do not really want to call in Omaha with a hand that cannot hit the nuts. But **You** may be winning and could hit a Five for a straight. If the high card were other than an Ace, you might have raised. Still better, you might have come out betting.

In Omaha you don't want to call to try to improve a hand which is not the nuts.

Action 4: You call $50.

The turn A♣7♦6♥5♣. **You** hold 8♣7♦6♥4♣. The pot is $157.
Both of **You** have $1000 left.

Note how much more comfortable the situation would be if **Gerald** were first to speak.

Position is nearly as important in Omaha as in Texas Hold 'em.

Question 5: Should **You** (a) check (b) bet $50 (c) bet $100 (d) bet $157?
Answer 5: (a) 6 (b) 2 (c) 4 (d) 10
Reason 5: You have made a straight, but it is not the nuts. **You** have also made a *backdoor* club flush draw. That is quite nice. If you check and **Gerald** bets, **You** won't know where **You** stand. A small bet would be messy. If he calls, **You** still won't know where **You** stand.
Action 5: You bet $150 and **Gerald** calls.

The river A♣7♦6♥5♣5♥. **You** hold 8♣7♦6♥4♣. The pot is $457.

Question 6: Should **You** (a) check (b) bet $150 (c) bet $300 (d) bet $450?
Answer 6: (a) 10 (b) 2 (c) 0 (d) 0
Reason 6: A testing bet is not too bad. But, if **Gerald** recognizes it as such, he is not going to call, and may raise without a full house. It is best to check and make a decision later, if **Gerald** bets.
Action 6: You check. **Gerald** bets $350. The pot is $807.

Question 7: Should **You** (a) pass (b) call (c) raise $350 (d) raise $500 all-in?
Answer 7: (a) 10 (b) 7 (c) 0 (d) 0
Reason 7: Gerald must have had some type of hand in order to call on the turn. It may have been the nut straight, or the same straight as you hold or trips.
Action 7: You pass and we will never know whether it was the correct decision.

This shows how complicated Omaha can be. It shouldn't be your first form of poker, except against other novices.

Score:	
70	You are reading this book under false pretences. You are not a beginner.
60-69	Still pretty amazing.
50-59	Very good.
40-49	Still acceptable.
30-39	You are not ready to play for money yet.
20-29	Reread the material.
10-19	Are you sure you have grasped the basic concept?
-3 to 9	You must try to understand all the opportunities.

The wrap concept

Flop	Holding	No. of cards to make a straight	No. of cards to make the nut straight	Odds against making a straight by the river
A♣9♦8♠	J♥10♥7♦6♠	20	14	3/7
A♣9♦8♠	J♦10♠7♣5♦	17	11	2/3
A♣9♦8♠	10♥7♠6♥4♥	17	7	2/3
A♣9♦8♠	Q♦J♣10♣7♥	16	16	2/3
A♣9♦8♠	K♦Q♣J♠10♦	13	13	Evens
A♣9♦8♠	7♠6♦5♥3♠	13	3	Evens
A♣9♦7♠	10♠8♦6♥4♣	17	11	2/3

A♣9♦7♠	J♥10♥8♣6♦	16	16	2/3
A♣9♦7♠	8♥6♣5♠4♦	13	3	Evens
A♣9♦6♥	10♥8♣7♦4♥	13	13	Evens
A♣9♦6♥	8♦7♥5♣4♠	13	7	Evens
A♣9♦6♥	8♥7♣4♣3♦	8	8	2/1
A♣9♦5♥	8♠7♥6♦4♥	9	9	7/4

A wrap is where you can make more than two straights. Whenever somebody tells you he had two pair and a wrap, you know he either doesn't know what he is talking about, or is having you on. Three cards are needed for any type of wrap.
Of course it is also possible to have a flush draw.

Flop	Holding	No. of cards to make a flush or straight	No. of cards to make the nut flush or straight	Odds to make a straight or flush by the river
J♣10♣4♦	K♣Q♣9♦8♦	25	12	1/4
J♣10♣4♦	A♣K♦Q♦9♣	22	22	1/3

The number of winning drawing cards you have is called the number of *outs*.You would think you had the most wonderful hand with 25 outs on the flop. But, if you come up against the second hand, your only way to win would be with a Seven other than that of clubs. Another point to remember is, that although the 4♣ gives you the flush, it may give your opponent a full house.

Remember you are trying to make the nuts in Omaha.

Making a hand on the last two cards, i.e. by the backdoor, is also possible in Texas hold 'em, but it is much more likely in Omaha.

The odds shown are not the probability of your winning the hand. Your opponent may make a full house or a backdoor flush.

OK, so you have some problem understanding these concepts or remembering the odds. Earmark the section and return to it time and again. Nor do you need to know the precise odds.

With two cards to come:

- You are an underdog with less than 13 outs
- You are even money to improve with 13 outs
- You are favorite to improve with more than 13 outs
- You are favorite to win against trips with 17 or more outs.

SAMPLE HAND 11

Lauren is in the small blind for $1 and **Sid** in the big blind for $2. **Joe** passes. The pot is $3 and **You** hold A♣9♦8♣6♦.

Question 1: Should **You** (a) pass (b) call (c) raise $2 (d) raise $5?

Answer 1: (a) 0 (b) 10 (c) 2 (d) 6

Reason 1: This is a pretty good hand. Were the 6♦ the 7♦, I would definitely raise. But in a tournament in the early stages I would just call. Why get involved when you have nothing so far?

Action 1: You call. **Ann** calls, **Stewart** raises $9, **Freda** raises $29, **Sid** calls.

The pot is $96 and it is $38 to **You**. There is about $1500 to be won from each opponent.

Question 2: Should **You** (a) pass (b) call (c) raise $40 (d) raise $100?

Answer 2: (a) 4 (b) 10 (c) 0 (d) 1

Reason 2: One of either **Freda** and **Stewart** probably has Aces. This reduces your hand effectively to three cards. But, since they cannot both have Aces, it is unlikely you will have to face two more raises before the flop.

Action 2: You call. **Ann** passes and **Stewart** reraises $100. **Freda** and **Sid** call.

The pot is $472. **You** hold A♣9♦8♣6♦.

Question 3: Should **You** (a) pass (b) call (c) raise $100 (d) raise $550?

Answer 3: (a) 2 (b) 10 (c) 0 (d) 0

Reason 3: You are actually getting better odds than last time around. Why does **Stewart** only raise $100? Perhaps he expected **Freda** to reraise. **You** have it fairly fixed in your mind that **Stewart** has Aces.
Action 3: You call.
The flop K♣7♣5♠. **You** hold A♣9♦8♣6♦. The pot is $572. **You** can see that **Freda** is raring to go and really intends to bet. **Sid** checks. **You** have $1350 left.

Question 4: Should **You** (a) check (b) bet $100 (c) bet $200 (c) bet $550?
Answer 4: (a) 10 (b) 0 (c) 0 (d) 4
Reason 4: If **You** can see somebody else getting ready to spring into action, there seems little point in doing anything other than check. Of course, sometimes you may be surprised and the other player is *moodying* and checks.
Action 4: You check. **Stewart** bets $100 and **Freda** does her duty and raises $750. **Sid** passes. The pot is $1522. It is **$850** to call and **You** have $1350 left.

Question 5: Should **You** (a) pass (b) call (c) raise $500 all-in?
Answer 5: (a) -2 (b) 10 (c) 5
Reason 5: You have a premium hand. Any club gives you the nut flush. Any 9, 8, 6 or 4 gives you the straight.

Question 6: How many outs do you have, not counting 5♣ (a) 14 (b) 16 (c) 18 (d) 20?
Answer 6: (a) 0 (b) 5 (c) 10 (d) 5 Go on, re-count them!

Returning to **Reason 5: You** are favorite against trips Kings. But there seems little point in reraising. **Stewart** might call and **You** don't want to discourage him. If **You** hit your hand, **Freda** will have to call the final bet if she has trips. Her odds will be too good to pass. Also, if an open pair comes, **You** can check and possibly pass if **Freda** bets.
Action 6: You call and **Stewart** passes. What was he doing, wasting $100 on a *gay bet*?

The turn K♣7♣5♠6♥. **You** hold A♣9♦8♣6♦. The pot is $2372. **You** have $500 left.
Question 7: Should **You** (a) check (b) bet $500 all-in?

Answer 7: (a) 0 (b) 10

Reason 7: Freda cannot pass, she is getting $2872/$500 = 11/2. She is only about 7/2 against hitting a full house. **You** would love her to pass, giving you a $2872 pot and no risk.

Action 7: You bet and **Freda** calls.

The river K♣7♣5♠6♥2♥. **You** hold A♣9♦8♣6♦. The pot is $3372. **Freda** held K♥K♠8♥4♠. **Your** hand wasn't quite as good as **You** thought, because **Freda** had two defensive cards. **I** claim **I** had A♥A♦8♥6♦, which removes two more cards. **You** apologize for getting so lucky and enjoy yourself re-stacking your chips for the next couple of minutes.

Score:	
70	You have got the hang of this game.
60-69	You probably go near the top of the class.
50-59	Not bad.
40-49	Satisfactory.
30-39	Not good.
20-29	Unsatisfactory.
10-19	Extremely mediocre.
-2 to 9	Spend your money on my other books rather than waste it on Omaha.

Limit Omaha

See pages 164 to 165 for full description of the betting system.

- Each bet or raise before the flop is $2.
- Each bet or raise on the flop is $2.
- Each bet or raise on the turn is $4.
- Each bet or raise on the river is $4.

You should play much tighter before the flop when facing the original bet or first raise in limit Omaha than in Pot Limit Omaha. Much the same is true of limit Texas hold 'em.

Your potential win is much smaller and it is so easy to get seduced by high pot odds into losing money. Thus hands such as:

Beware of danglers in Omaha. They can leave you swinging in the breeze.

A♥10♠8♦5♥ or J♣10♦9♣4♥ should be passed. In the former case you just have a nut flush draw and some weedy-looking straights.

In the second case, the 4♥ is a *dangler*. That is a card which bears no relationship to the other three.

SAMPLE HAND 12

This is a pot **I** really did play in Adelaide. Well, what better way could I have spent my one night in that attractive city than playing poker? I don't recall any of the names of the players. I was probably the only stranger in the game, but that cuts both ways.

The small blind bet $2, the big blind put in $4. Four players called.

I held K♦Q♣10♣10♦. The pot was $22.

Question 1: Should **I** have (a) passed (b) called (c) raised $4?
Answer 1: (a) -1 (b) 7 (d) 10
Reason 1: This is a completely co-ordinated, pretty good hand.
Action 1: I raised, the player after me called and so did five of the six players in the pot in front of me.

The flop 10♥7♦2♥. I held K♦Q♣10♣10♦. The pot was $54. Two players checked, one player bet and two others called. The pot was $66 and it was $4 to me.

Question 2: Should **I** have (a) passed (b) called (c) raised $4?
Answer 2: (a) -2 (b) 0 (c) 10
Reason 2: I have the nuts, nobody can be favorite against my hand and there is no need for disguise against such a large field.
Action 2: I raised $4. The player immediately after me called. The big blind called.

The next player raised $4 and the next two players called. The pot was $114.

Question 3: Should **I** have (a) passed (b) called (c) made the third and final raise of $4?
Answer 3: (a) -2 (b) 0 (c) 10
Reason 3: Nothing has changed.
Action 3: I raised $4. The other five players all called.
The turn 10♥7♦2♥J♠. **I** held K♦Q♣10♣10♦. The pot was $146.

The first player checked. The second player bet $8, the third player called $8, and the fourth player raised. The pot was $178. It was $16 to call.

Question 4: Should **I** have (a) passed (b) called (c) raised $8?
Answer 4: (a) 0 (b) 8 (c) 10
Reason 4: It is perfectly obvious two players had straights. It was going to cost me $32 to reach the river. My odds were therefore $194/$32 = 6/1. It is only about 2/1 against making a full house or top straight. Since I was going to put the money in, I should have disguised my hand by raising, pretending that I too had a straight.
Action 4: I called. The man after me called. The first player passed. The first bettor raised $8, the next player called, the second raiser made the final raise to $16. The pot was $248.

Question 5: Should I have (a) passed (b) called?
Answer 5: (a) -2 (b) 10
Reason 5: Well, if you didn't get that one right, you really haven't been following the story.
Action 5: I called as did the mystery man after me. The first raiser called and so did the middle-man. The pot was $296.

The river 10♥7♦2♥J♠10♠. I held K♦Q♣10♣10♦.

The first player bet $8. The middle man called. The next player raised $8. The pot was $328 and it was $16 to me.

Question 6: Should **I** have (a) passed (b) called (c) raised to $24?
Answer 6: (a) -5 (b) 4 (c) 10
Reason 6: I seriously contemplated not raising for about one second. How on earth was **I** going to get paid with the obvious quads?
Action : I made it $24 to go. I nearly fell off my chair when the only player on my right put in the final raise to $32. The original bettor said, "Well, everybody knows what I have," and passed. The first raiser said, "Well, I have to call for value." The pot was $400.

Question 7: Should **I** have (a) passed (b) called?
Answer 7: (a) -5 (b) 10
Reason 7: As **I** called, a player, not in the pot, whispered, "It's Christmas!"
Action 7: Thus **I** won a $408 pot in a $2 $4 game. Eventually the player to my left explained that he had J♥J♦, i.e. the nut full house and had momentarily forgotten that I could have quads. He never explained how he got into the hand—and anyway may have lied. You are allowed to do that in poker. Later that evening I was told this was the biggest hand ever seen at that limit in Adelaide.

Score:	
70	This should have been the easiest quiz of all.
60-69	Very good.
50-59	Acceptable.
40-49	You should be more aggressive.
30-39	Unsatisfactory.
20-29	You don't understand Omaha—yet.
10-19	Rather poor.
17-9	Better luck next time.

Seven card stud

I used to be recognized as the best player in the world at this game when played Pot Limit. That isn't all that great, since it was not played at all in the United States and even in Europe it is only played for small stakes. This is a great pity as it is highly skilful. Thus we will concentrate on the Limit game, which is still popular, especially in the U.S. and on the internet.

1. Each player *antes* $1. There is a maximum of eight players.

2. Each player receives two cards face down and one face up.

3. The low card must *bring it in* for $2, or could open for $5. If there are two cards of the same denomination showing, then the suit order goes from lowest to highest, ♣♦♥♠ just like in bridge.

4. Each raise is first to make it up to $5 and then raise a further $5.

5. The betting goes around the table just like in Texas Hold 'em or Omaha.

6. While there are more than two players in the pot, the maximum number of raises is three.

7. If nobody has raised, the low card has no more rights than anybody else. He cannot reopen the betting as he has already bet.

8. When the money has been equalized, a fourth card is dealt face up to each player remaining. This is called fourth street or the turn.

9. From now on it is the high hand which must act first.

10. The highest two card hand has the option of checking or betting $5.

11. Each raise is again $5

12. After the money is equalized, a fifth card is dealt to each player face up. Would you believe, it is called fifth street.

13. From now on all bets and raises are $10.

14. Once the money is equalized, a sixth card is dealt face up. This is *sixth street*. Should everybody still be in the pot at this stage there will not be enough cards left to go round. In that case, one last card is dealt face up in the centre of the table and is a communal card that can be used by any player.

15. Once the money is equalized, a seventh card is dealt face down. This is called seventh street or, more commonly the river as in Texas Hold 'em or Omaha.

16. Once the money is equalized the best hand claims the pot.

If you plot it through, you will find there is one more betting interval in Seven Stud than in Texas Hold 'em or Omaha. Thus a Seven Stud game tends to be bigger than an equivalent Texas Hold 'em or Omaha game. One effect of this was that, when played Pot Limit, there was seldom enough money left for a bet on the river and players did not like this.

SAMPLE HAND 13

We will keep this first hand really simple and restrict it to two players.

You are low card with (9♥9♣) 3♦. You bring it in for $2 and the next six players fold, passing 8♥, 7♠, Q♦, 4♦, 8♣, 3♥. **I** hold **(??) K♠.** You note, this is a game of greater information than the flop games.

Each player can of course see only his own two hole cards. So far I have yet to look at my cards, but you, of course, wouldn't normally know that.

Action: I make it $10. That is correct bluffing play. **You** may have absolutely nothing. Many players believe a player should always raise in this position. I disagree. But a King is a stronger than average card. The pot is $20.

Question 1: Should **You** (a) pass (b) call for $8 (c) raise $5?
Answer 1: (a) 0 (b) 4 (c) 10
Reason 1: You have quite a strong hand at this stage.
Action 1: You raise $5. Now **I** look at my hole cards and find (10♠Q♣) K♠.

The pot is $33. It is $5 to me.

Question 2: Should **I** (a) pass (b) call (c) raise $5?
Answer 2: (a) 2 (b) 10 (c) 0
Reason 2: Received wisdom is that one should call with three *live over-cards* in this situation. Live means when you haven't seen many of them on the table. In this case there is just the Q♦ passed. Also I do have the making of a straight, although **I** will need to hit a Jack. Again note how important it is to keep track of the cards.
Action: I call.

Fourth street **You** (9♥9♣) 3♦6♦. **I** (10♠Q♣) K♠ J♠. The pot is $38. Remember we do not know each other's cards.

Question 3: Should I: (a) check (b) bet $5?
Answer 3: (a) 10 (b) 10
Reason 3: Well, at least in this quiz you are not going to score zero! **I** have a strong hand. Four to an up and down straight with no nines or Aces showing is even money to make it with three cards to come. But **I** might bet with the idea of giving the impression that I have now hit a pair of Jacks. Alternatively **I** might check with the intention of raising if **You** bet.
Action 3: I bet $5. The pot is $43. **You** (9♥9♣) 3♦6♦. **I** (??) K♠J♠ from your viewpoint.

Question 4: Should **You** (a) pass (b) call (c) raise $5?
Answer 4: (a) 0 (b) 10 (c) 0
Reason 4: You have 43/5 for your money. **You** may well be winning against a four flush and your hand is disguised because **You** have two diamonds showing. There is no way **I** intend to pass after betting. A raise would be senseless.
Action 4: You call.

Fifth street **You** (9♥9♣) 3♦6♦3♠. **I** (10♠Q♣) K♠J♠10♥. The pot is $48.

Question 5: Should **You** (a) check (b) bet $10?
Answer 5: (a) 0 (b) 10
Reason 5: You are probably winning and why give a free card?
Action 5: You bet $10. The pot is $58.

Question 6: Should **I** (a) pass (b) call (c) raise $10?
Answer 6: (a) 0 (b) 10 (c) 2
Reason 6: It is always worrying when somebody pairs his *door card*. That is his first up card. If a player starts with a pair, it is twice as likely for him to have paired his door card rather than have a pair in the hole. Thus it is possible **You** have trips, or even a full house. But remember the 3♥ passed at the start? **You** might have passed a hand like (7♣3♣) 3♦. The cards are very dead. Looking at it more optimistically, **You** may have a four flush and a pair.
Action 6: I call.

Sixth street **You** (9♥9♣) 3♦6♦3♠9♠. **I** (10♠Q♣) K♠J♠10♥Q♥. The pot is $68.

Question 7: Should **You** (a) check (b) bet $10?
Answer 7: (a) 2 (b) 10
Reason 7: There is no need to slowplay your hand. Few people call on fifth street and pass on sixth. *Trap checking*, intending to raise if **I** bet is less powerful. It would probably just be giving a free card.

Action 7: You bet $10. The pot is $78.

Question 8: Should **I** (a) pass (b) call (c) raise $10?
Answer 8: (a) 0 (b) 6 (c) 10
Reason 8: This is a pretty good two pair. It is unlikely **You** have more than two pair.
Action 8: I raise. **You** raise $10. The pot is $108.

Question 9: Should **I** (a) pass (b) call (c) raise $10?
Answer 9: (a) 0 (b) 10 (c) 0
Reason 9: Even if **You** just have trip threes or Aces up, **You** are winning. If **You** have a full house, **I** can still improve. It is about 10/1 against my making a full house. **I** should win two more bets if **I** *fill up*, that is make a full house.
Action 9: I call.

The river **You** (9♥9♣A♦) 3♦6♦3♠9♠. **I** (10♠Q♣A♣) K♠J♠10♥Q♥. The pot is $118.

Question 10: Should **You** (a) check (b) bet $10?
Reason 10: It seems likely **I** am going to call.
Action 10: You bet. The pot is $128.

Question 11: Should **I** (a) pass (b) call (c) raise $10?
Answer 11: (a) 0 (b) 10 (c) 6
Reason 11: Even if I believe **You** almost certainly hold a full house, I must make a *crying call*, which is one made where you think you are losing, but cannot resist the odds. 14/1 odds is too good to pass up. If **I** don't believe **you** have a full house, then a raise is in order.

Action 11: I call $10 with my straight and **You** show down a full house.

Score:	
110	How long did you say you had been playing Seven Card Stud?
90-109	A very good effort.
70-89	Not at all bad.
50-69	You haven't got the hang of the game yet.
30-49	Perhaps the game will click for you later.
10-29	Perhaps I haven't explained the game adequately.
0-9	Reread the entire section.

SAMPLE HAND 14

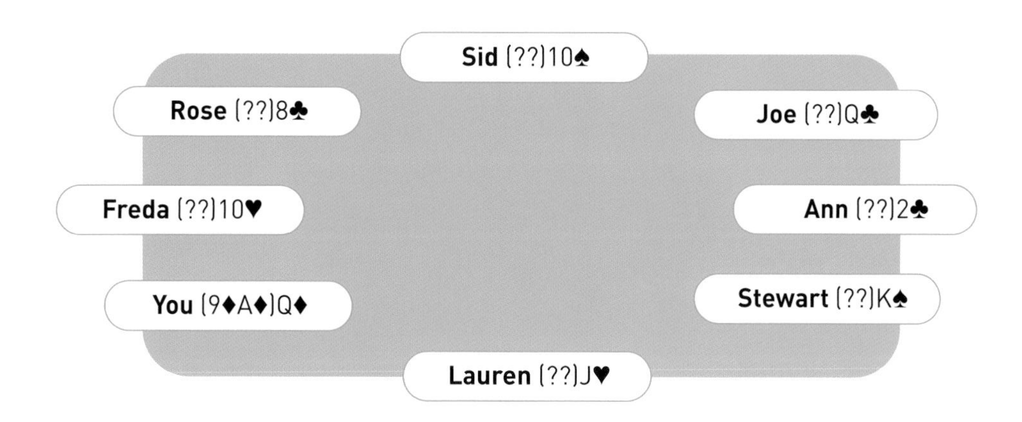

Everybody antes $1. **Ann** brings it for $2 being the low card. **Stewart** calls. **Lauren** makes it $10. The pot is $22 and it is $10 to **You**.

Question 1: Should **You** (a) pass (b) call (c) raise $10?
Answer 1: (a) 0 (b) 10 (c) 3
Reason 1: Three to a flush, with no diamonds showing is a strong drawing hand, especially holding an Ace. However, it is a drawing hand and **You** prefer more players in the pot.
Action 1: You call as do **Freda** and **Joe**. **Stewart** raises $5. **Lauren** calls. The pot is $70.

I played poker for some weeks in Las Vegas in 1974, but did not return for five years. The first game I sat in I played a hand in exactly this manner, first calling with the high card and then back-raising. Billy King exclaimed, "He still plays exactly the same way as five years ago!" English players were much more a novelty at that time than today.

Question 2: Should **You** (a) pass (b) call $5 (c) raise $5?
Answer 2: (a) 0 (b) 10 (c) 2
Reason 2: Really nothing has changed.
Action 2: You call as do **Freda** and **Joe**.

Fourth street

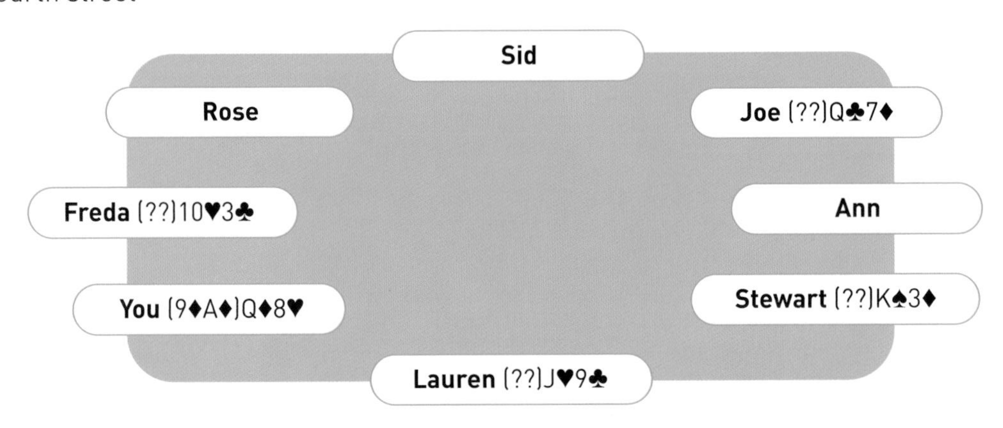

Stewart bets $5. **Lauren** calls. The pot is $95 and it is $5 to **You**.

Question 3: Should **You** (a) pass (b) call (c) raise $5?
Answer 3: (10) (b) 8 (c) 0. **You** do not perceive anybody as gearing themselves up to raise.
Reason 3: You have encountered one of the perennial problems of a stud player. You had an excellent drawing card, but now it has busted out. Perceived wisdom is that **You** should pass unless the hand has been triple bet. Here you have a completely live Ace and don't particularly fear being back-raised.
Action 3: You call, **Freda** passes and **Joe** calls.

Fifth street. The pot is $105 and **You** are high.

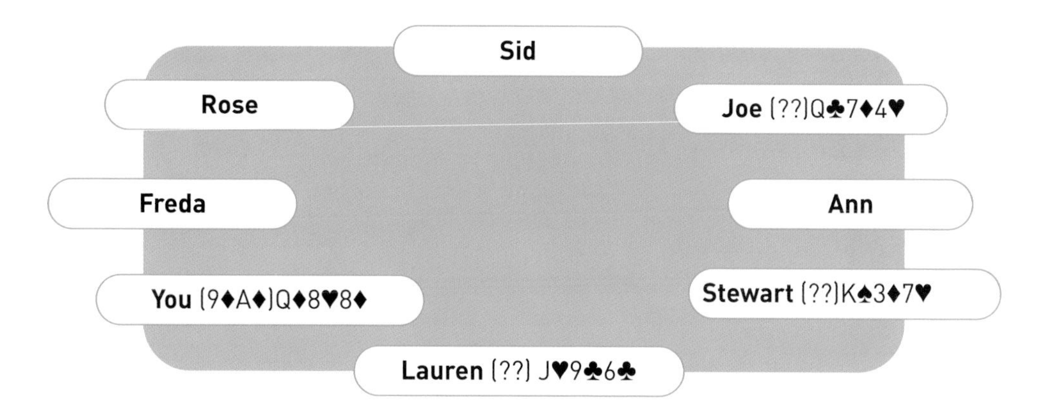

Question 4: Should **You** (a) check (b) bet $10?
Answer 4: (a) 5 (b) 10
Reason 4: Now **You** have a good four flush, **You** have bought your ticket to the river. A four flush plus a pair is an excellent hand with two cards to come.
Action 4: You bet $10 and **Joe** passes. **Stewart** raises $10. **Lauren** flat calls $20. The pot is $155 and it is $10 to **You**.

Question 5: Should **You** (a) pass (b) call (c) raise $10?
Answer 5: (a) -2 (b) 7 (c) 10
Reason 5: Stewart doesn't have to have a monster of a hand to raise. He may have been trying to put pressure on **Lauren** to get her out. This hasn't worked. If **You** raise and **Stewart** puts in the last raise, **Lauren** is unlikely to wilt and pass. But **You** will getting 2/1 for any extra money you wager and that is not at all bad with this drawing hand. After all, **You** may hit an Ace or Eight and win the pot. Reraising disguises your hand and suggests **You** have more than one pair.
Action 5: You raise $10 and **Stewart** and **Lauren** call. The pot is $185.

Sixth Street

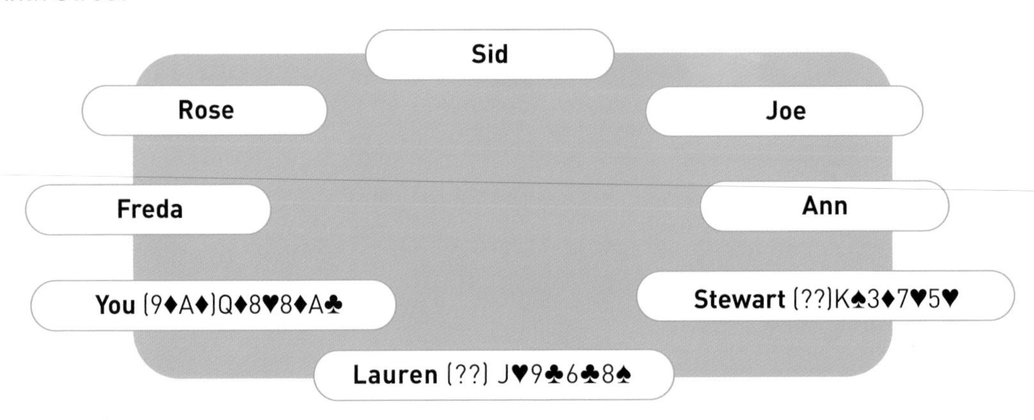

Question 6: Should **You** (a) check (b) bet $10?
Answer 6: (a) 3 (c) 10
Reason 6: There is little reason to expect a bet if **You** check. **You** are probably winning.
Action 6: You bet $10, **Stewart** calls and **Lauren** raises $10. The pot is $225.

Question 7: Should **You** (a) pass (b) call (c) raise $10?
Action 7: (a) 0 (b) 9 (c) 10
Reason 7: Obviously neither of them believes **You** have a full house with only one Eight left, but isn't **Your** Aces up winning? Even if not, **You** have a tremendously good draw. There are no Aces showing and only one diamond. If **You** raise, then **Stewart** may well pass. That would mean **You** will have isolated yourself with the best hand. What does **Lauren** hold? The most likely explanation is (Q-10)J♥9♣6♣8♠. Well, **You** can outdraw a straight, **You** have 11 cards to beat that.
Action 7: You raise $10 and **Stewart** calls. **Lauren** makes the final raise. The pot is $275 and it is $10 to **You**.

Question 8: Should **You** (a) pass (b) call?
Answer 8: (a) -5 (b) 10
Reason: I do hope everybody got that one right.
Action 8: You call.

The river. The pot is $285.

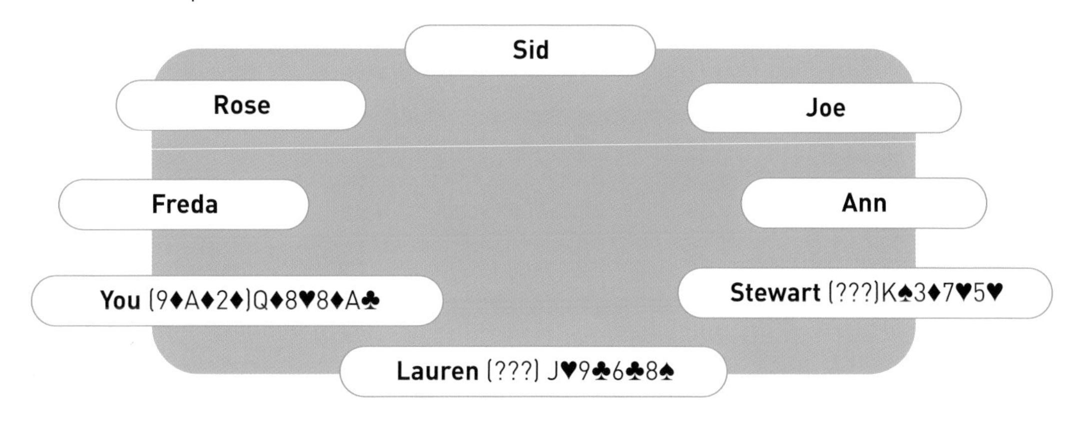

Question 9: Should **You** (a) check (b) bet $10?

Answer 9: (a) 10 (b) 7

Reason 9: If **You** check, **Lauren** is almost certain to bet.

Action 9: You check as does **Stewart**. **Lauren** bets $10. The pot is $295.

Question 10: Should **You** (a) pass (b) call (c) raise $10?

Answer 10: (a) -5 (b) 5 (c) 10

Reason 10: You are almost certainly winning and **Stewart** may not call even $10. **Lauren** is certain to call with $315 in the pot.

Action 10: You raise $10. **Stewart** passes and **Lauren** calls. The pot is $335.

You win. **Lauren** bemoans her luck, but should she have called on fifth street to make a hand which had such poor chances? As you will have guessed, **Stewart** did have Kings up. There was too much money in the pot to pass on sixth street.

That is the problem with Aces or Kings, they tend to win small pots or lose big ones.

You will note it is important to know all the passed cards. What if you forget, or get it wrong? That will happen from time to time, just don't include them in your reckoning.

FINER POINTS

At its finest, poker is very much a game of representation and bluffing. When you start out it is much more likely to be a matter of avoiding over-betting your hand and calling with inadequate odds.

Bluffing

- It is very hard to bluff out an inexperienced opponent. That is why this never came up in our sample hands.
- The more players in the pot, the harder it is to run a bluff.
- Opponents who are level are easier to bluff than winners or losers.
- A *check-raise* usually represents a very strong hand.
- People who have a little something are less likely to bluff.
- People who are about to leave are easier to bluff.
- Opponents who seem inattentive are usually weak, but sometimes are strong.
- If you are thinking of calling a bluff, it may be best to raise.

Usually your opponents will want to call. They are looking for reasons to call, not to pass.

Categories of players

Poker players have often been put into four categories.

1. Weak loose. These are the easiest to beat. They simply call with inadequate odds and seldom raise. Thus they fail to protect their moderately good hands and fail to capitalize on their good fortune. Blessed are they, but they will not inherit the money.

2. Weak tight. These players lose their money more slowly than our first category. But they are the easiest to play against. If they call, simply switch off, unless you are winning.

3. Hard loose. You will lose most money to these players and hopefully win even more. They won't hesitate to raise if they think they can win. Often you will come seriously unstuck when they have a hand even better than yours.

4. Hard tight. These are virtually impregnable. They pick their battlegrounds with care and will not hesitate to bet or raise when it fits the situation. Equally, they won't be reluctant to pass.

Of course, ideally you want to change your styles during the session. But the problem is that you can only give the impression of being weak loose by playing in that losing fashion. It might be a good idea to play hard tight for a time and then switch to hard loose for the next period.

Odds

I have quoted a number of odds in certain situations without trying to justify the statement. This is because many people reading this may not know anything about the maths of probability.

If the pot is $30 and it costs you $15 to call, you have 2/1 odds for your money. Similarly if it is $10, the odds are 3/1. For $3 it is 10/1. With one card to come:

$$\text{Your odds against improving} = \frac{\text{Number of cards left that do not help}}{\text{Number of cards that do help you}}$$

In the last sample Seven Card Stud hand, there were 11 cards with which you would win. You have seen 22 cards. Thus there were 30 left. The odds against winning = (30-11)/1 which is 7/4. You can happily raise, provided two opponents call.

Of course some of the cards you want will already have been passed, or may lie with your opponents. You should assume they are all available.

It becomes more sophisticated when you realize that you may make your hand, only for an opponent to make a better one. This is particularly true of Omaha. It also happens in Seven Stud where you cannot see what your opponent has hit on the river.

When there are two or more cards to come, the odds against your improving, and your opponent not also improving even more, become extremely complex. Often the easiest thing to do is put the information into a computer and have it deal out a million hands. This is not practical at the poker table!

You do not have to know the answers, nor to work them out at the table. There are poker books or software which can provide the answers. Below are a few simple examples:

	Situation	Opponent	You	Odds against
Hold 'em	Preflop	A♣A♦	K♠K♥	9/2
Hold 'em	Flop A♦9♣6♥	A♣Q♥	8 ♠7♣	2/1
Hold 'em	Flop A♦9♦6♥	A♣Q♥	K♦5♦	13/7
	Flop A♦9♦6♥	A♣Q♥	8♦7♦	5/6
Omaha	Preflop	Aces + 2 cards	8♦7♦6♣5♣	3/2
Omaha	Flop 10♠5♦3♠	Tens + 2 cards	A♠Q♠9♥6♥	3/1
Omaha	Flop J♠10♦3♣	Jacks + 2 cards	A♥K♦Q♠6♥	3/2
Omaha	Flop J♠10♦3♣	Jacks + 2 cards	A♥K♦Q♠9♥	11/10
Seven Stud	Fourth street	A♥A♠9♣4♦	K♥J♥8♥6♥	Evens
Seven Stud	Fourth street	A♥A♠9♣4♦	Q♥J♥10♦9♠	Evens

POKER TERMS

There are many technical words and terms in poker, many of which are italicized in the text. Below are explanations to help you understand these terms.

All-in Where a player has run out of money during a hand but not passed.

Ante Where all the players put in the same sum of money, the ante, before the cards are dealt. Texas Hold 'em and Omaha can be played this way, but this is not discussed in this book.

Backdoor Where you make a hand other than the one you first aimed for, due to cards that came later.

Bet A wager.

Big bet In limit, the size of the bet on the turn or river.

Big blind The secondary mandatory bet in Texas hold 'em or Omaha.

Blank A card which seems to help nobody.

Blind Betting without seeing one's cards.

Bluffing Making a bet or raise in a hope of winning the pot, not in expectation of having the superior hand.

Board The cards showing which are in play.

Brick wall A situation where you have little hope.

Bring it in Make the first bet in a given round.

Buck A disc to represent the dealer. Action always takes place after the buck in flop games.

Burnt card The top card left in the deck is discarded or "burnt". This is to help prevent cheating.

Button See buck.

Buy-in The amount of money a player starts with.

Call To match the amount of money the previous bettor has wagered.

Check To take no betting action at this stage; often indicated by knocking on the table.

Check-raise To check originally and then, when somebody else bets, to raise.

Chip Plastic discs where each color represents a certain amount of money.

Connectors Two, three, or four cards in sequence.

Crying call Calling where you think you are losing, but cannot resist the odds.

Dangler A card in Omaha which bears no relationship to the other three.

Deal The process of giving the players cards, or laying cards in the centre.

Deck A set of 52 playing cards.

Door card In Stud, a player's first up-card.

Drawing Where you are calling a bet in the hope of being dealt card(s) which will win you the pot.

Favorite A hand more likely to win than those opposing it.

Fifth Street The round of betting after the fifth card is dealt in Seven Stud, or occasionally, after the river card is dealt in Texas Hold 'em or Omaha.

Fill up Make a full house.

Flop The three communal cards placed face up in the centre of the table in Texas Hold 'em or Omaha.

Flush Five cards of the same suit.

Fourth Street The round of betting after the fourth card is dealt in Seven Stud, or occasionally, after the turn card is dealt in Texas Hold 'em or Omaha.

Free card One, because nobody else has bet, that comes free.

Full house Three of a kind plus two of a kind.

Gambling Either wagering, or wagering against the odds.

Gay bet A small bet which reopens the betting for other players.

Go to the table Go all-in.

Hand The cards a player holds, or the whole action in the pot from deal to showdown.

Hole cards The cards a player holds which other players cannot see until the showdown.

Implied odds The money you are likely to win by further betting, if you make your hand.

Kicker The second card a player holds in addition to a pair made with one of the communal cards.

Kill the action To bet or raise all-in, so that there can be no further play.

Limit You can only bet or raise a certain pre-specified amount, which is usually much smaller than the pot.

Limp in To call a small bet.

Live cards Cards not seen on the table in Seven Stud.

Loose Calling with a hand that is unlikely to win.

Made hand Where you have a hand which may be winning.

Marginal hand One where the hand may be either in front or behind.

Matching cards Where two or more players have the same denomination card(s).

Middle-pin Such as 8 when you hold 10-9-7-6.

Moodying To misrepresent your hand by your mannerisms or talk.

Morton's Fork Where you are certain to have a hand which is either the best made hand or the best drawing one.

No Limit Where a player may bet or raise any amount when it is his turn.

Nuts The best hand at that stage of the pot.

Odds The amount you can win divided by the amount you must wager.

Omaha A game where each player has four cards and there are five communal cards.

Outs The number of cards you can hit to give you the winning hand.

Over-cards Cards you can hit which may match your cards and possibly give you a better hand than your opponent.

Pass To throw away one's hand. Careful! In the U.S. it is often synonymous with check.

Playing the board In Texas Hold 'em just using the five communal cards for your hand.

Position Where you are in the betting sequence among the players. This never changes in a particular hand in Texas Hold 'em or Omaha, but may in Seven Stud.

Pot Limit At any stage you may only bet, or raise up to the size of the pot after you have called.

Premium hand One that is likely to be winning.

Pot The money or chips at stake in the game.

Quads Four of a kind.

Raise To wager more than the previous bettor.

Reopen the betting To bet or raise so that other players can reraise.

River The last card dealt.

Round The stage where each player still in the pot matches the amount of money each other player has wagered.

Setting you in To bet all an opponent's remaining money.

Shopping the business Reveals the nature of one's hand.

Short stack A player who has fewer chips than some others at the table.

Side pot Everybody is in for the main pot. A side pot is between players who have more chips than somebody all-in.

Small blind The first mandatory bet in Texas Hold 'em or Omaha. It starts the action.

Seven Stud A game where each player eventually has three down cards and four showing.

Spread To provide a particular poker variation.

Stack The chips you hold.

Straight Five cards in a sequence.

Stud A game where each player has down cards and four cards showing.

Texas Hold 'em A game where each player has two cards and there are five communal cards.

Ticket to the river A hand you intend to play right to the end.

Tight player One who only plays really strong hands.

Tourists Players who have mediocre hands.

Tournament Where everybody puts in the same amount of money at the start. Play proceeds until one player has all the chips. The money is then divided by a pre-announced system, depending on when players are knocked out.

Trap checking Checking with the intention of raising if somebody else bets.

Trips Three cards of the same denomination.

Turn The fourth communal card dealt face up in Texas Hold 'em or Omaha.

Under-bet To bet less than the pot or the previous bet.

Underdog A hand which has only a poor chance of winning.

Whip-lashed To be bet at first from the right-hand side and then from the left.

Wrap In Omaha where you can make more than two straights.

CHAPTER 10

Other Games

This collection includes a number of games that didn't fit easily in the other sections, but that's not to say there aren't some great card games to play. Oh hell! is a good introduction to the trumps and trickery of Whist and Bridge, and Cribbage has been around for hundreds of years, so try your hand at it and see if you can work out the secret of its long life. If you're going to try Casino, make sure you're quick at numbers and combinations. And if you try out Tut! make sure you're playing with someone who'll forgive you if you win all the time!

Oh Hell!

PLAYERS: THREE OR MORE
DECK: FULL
SCORE SHEET: YES
ORIGIN: ENGLAND
SIMPLICITY FACTOR: 8
SKILL FACTOR: 8
SUITABLE FOR CHILDREN: 8
SUITABLE FOR GAMBLING: 6

Sometimes, for obvious reasons, called Oh Well!, this is a pretty straightforward Whist-based game for upwards of three players that contains a couple of interesting twists.

In every deal the amount of cards dealt to each player goes up by one, so the first hand consists of one card, the second two, the third three, and so on, until it can't be raised, which signifies the end of the game. If there are three players there will be seventeen hands, four players thirteen hands, etc. After each deal, the first card of the remainder is turned over to signify trumps, but, in the case of, say, a four-player game where there will be no remainder on the final hand, it is played as No Trumps.

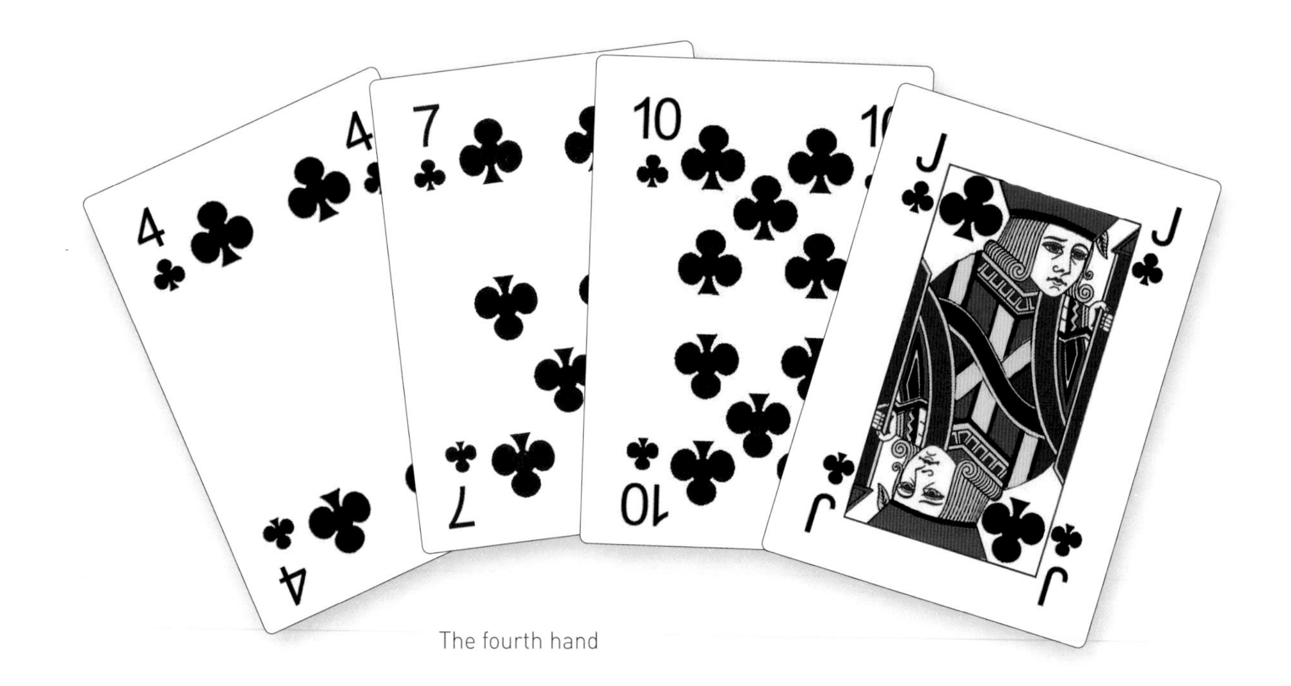

The fourth hand

Once the hands have been dealt, players bid for how many tricks they think they'll take—if it is none, as it may well be in the earlier rounds, they must declare "Nullo". Scores are kept cumulatively, and totaled up at the end of the game.

SCORING

At the end of each hand, the players that make their contract exactly score one point per trick and a ten-point bonus; players who go either over or under their contracted number of tricks score no points but do not incur any penalty. For making a contracted nullo, a player will score one point per trick in that hand, plus a ten-point bonus.

It might seem like a good idea to declare "nullo" as often as possible, and so win your bonus points each time for meeting your contract. In practice you'll find the other players will probably try to force you to take a trick or two if they can. Bear in mind too, that if you have won your tricks, the other players may similarly join forces against you.

BETTING

A cash-for-points system should be worked out before the game begins, with the losers paying the winner the differences between their hands and his.

Did you know?

Also known as Nomination Whist, Weetabix or Bust. Oh Hell! is thought to have been devised by Geoffrey Mott-Smith in 1937. It is a simple game to learn but offers plenty of opportunity to develop trick taking techniques and is a good introduction to the more complicated game of Bridge.

Casino

PLAYERS: TWO TO FOUR

DECK: FULL

SCORE SHEET: YES

ORIGIN: ENGLAND

ACES: LOW IN PLAYING, HIGH SCORING

SIMPLICITY FACTOR: 10

SKILL FACTOR: 3

SUITABLE FOR CHILDREN: 7

SUITABLE FOR GAMBLING: 8

To play this medieval French game, it helps if you're good at maths, as it's all about finding as many combinations of numbers as quickly as you can. Sometimes spelled Cassino, it can be played with two, three or four players and used to be very popular in casinos with players playing against the bank.

Four cards are dealt, face-down and in pairs, to each player. After the dealer has dealt to himself, four cards are dealt, again in pairs, in a face-up row in the middle of the table. These extra cards are known as the "layout". The player to the dealer's left then tries to "capture" as many cards as possible from the layout by matching them, numerically, with cards in his hand. He does this by placing the card from his hand, face-down, on top of the card it matches. For instance, if the player holds the eight of clubs and the eight of hearts is showing in the layout, the player puts his eight of clubs face-down on the eight of hearts, removes it from the layout and places this trick in front of him.

The player can also capture tricks if a combination of cards showing in the layout numerically equals a card in his hand. For example, if the five of spades, the ace of clubs and the two of diamonds were in the layout they would add up to eight (aces count as one) and so could be "captured" by an eight to make a trick.

More than one capture can also be performed in tandem. For example, if the layout comprised the eight of hearts, five of spades, ace of clubs and two of diamonds, the eight of clubs could be used to make both captures simultaneously. In this case, all four layout cards would be gathered together

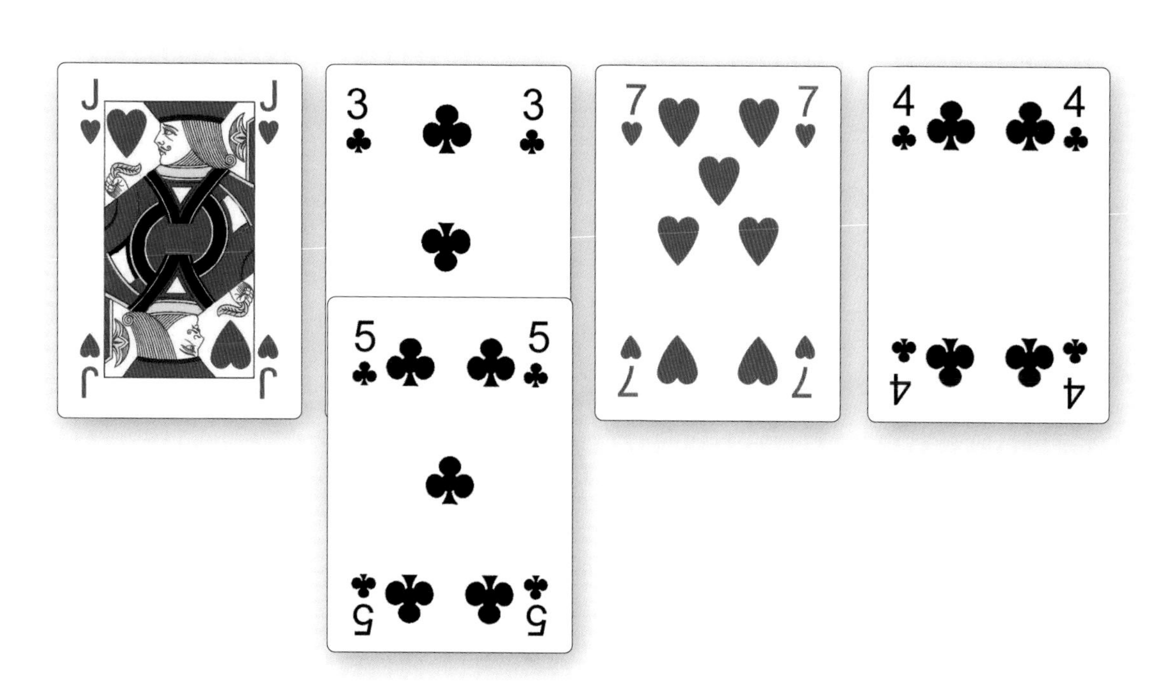

The eight can capture the three and five build

and the eight of clubs placed face-down on top to form one fat trick. To take all four cards in one capture is called a "sweep". Court cards can only be captured as pairs or when three of one denomination are in the layout and the player making the capture holds the fourth.

When tricks are gathered in, it's important the card that made the capture remains face-down with the others face-up, as in the scoring system only captured cards score points. Also, any sweeps made must be identifiable at the end.

As an alternative to straight captures, players can make "builds". Building involves laying cards from their hands face-up on layout cards, to make a total that adds up to a card in their hand, with the intention of capturing it next time around. For example, if the layout shows the three of hearts and the player holds the five of clubs and the eight of spades, he would put his five face-up on the table next to the three, announce that he was "building eight" and capture it with his eight on his next turn. However, his build is open to attack from other players who, if they can, may build on top of it. If the next player has a two and a ten in his hand, he could put the two down, face-up, next to the five, announce he is "building ten" and wait for it to come around to make the capture. But if the next player along also has a ten then that capture could be his. The more players involved in a game, the riskier building becomes.

Players can create "multiple builds" by building on two layout cards or existing builds with the aim of capturing them both with the same card held in their hand. If a player holds an eight, a two, a four and a king and the layout shows a four and a build that totals six, he can announce "building eights" (note the plural). He will then move his two targets next to each other, build the four on the other four and his two on the build of six and wait for his next turn to capture both tricks. Tripartite multiple builds are also possible. Although each aspect of multiple builds can continue to be built on, once announced the value cannot be changed.

Once a player has started a build, on his next turn he must capture that build, add to another one or start a new one. If he can't then he adds one of the cards from his hand face-up as part of the layout. As soon as all the players have played all the cards in their hand, they are dealt another four (once again in pairs) but no more cards are

added to the layout. Each new deal is called a "round" and a game will last for six rounds. When all the players have played all their cards on the sixth round, the player who made the most recent capture picks up the remaining layout cards and the scores are counted. The player with the most points wins the game.

SCORING

Only captured cards score points.

- If a player has captured more than 26 cards (half the deck) they score 3.
- Seven captured spades (of any denomination)—1.
- Each sweep made—1.
- Each ace captured—1.
- 10 of diamonds (known as "Big Casino")—2.
- Ace of spades ("Little Casino")—1.

Variations

DRAW CASINO

Instead of waiting for each player to play out their four cards before everybody is dealt new cards, players replenish their hands by drawing from the pot as they go along, and the game is played until the pot is exhausted.

SPADE CASINO

In this version, the ace, jack and two of spades are worth two points each; every other captured spade is worth one point.

CASINO ROYALE

The court cards have a value—kings 13, queens 12 and jacks 11—allowing them to be captured and used as part of builds.

Bouillotte

PLAYERS: THREE TO FIVE

DECK: 24 CARDS AT MOST

SCORE SHEET: NO

ACES: HIGH

ORIGIN: FRANCE

SIMPLICITY FACTOR: 9

SKILL FACTOR: 9

SUITABLE FOR CHILDREN: 7

SUITABLE FOR GAMBLING: 8

This is the game that Poker is believed to have evolved from when it was taken to the U.S. by French settlers. It is played with three, four or five players.

For three players the deck is reduced to ace, king, 9, 8; for four, ace, king, queen, jack, 9, 8; and for five it is ace, king, queen, jack, 9, 8, 7. Each player is dealt three cards and the top card (the "retourne") of the remainder is upturned in the centre of the table to be used by all players for scoring combinations. All players then compare hands, involving the retourne if necessary.

SCORING

In descending order, the hands are ranked as follows: four of a kind using the retourne ("brelan carré"); three of a kind not using the retourne ("brelan simple") and three of a kind using the retourne ("brelan favori"). If nobody is holding a brelan, the player holding the highest card wins.

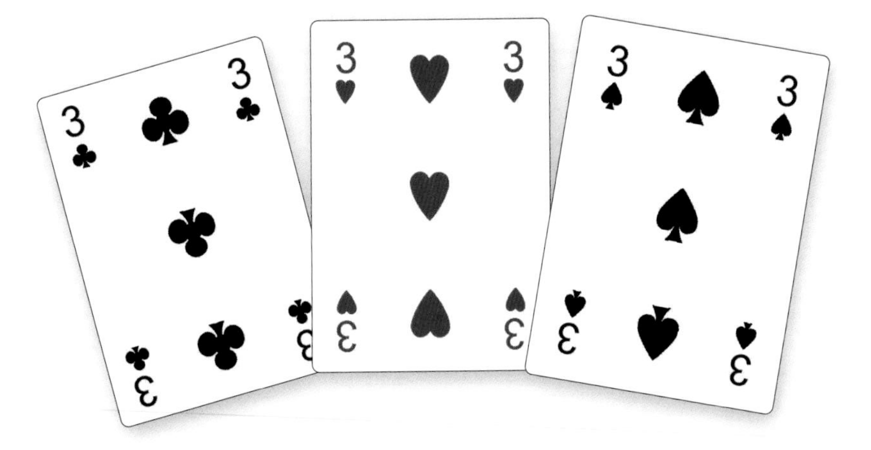

BETTING

After players have looked at their hands, betting goes in rounds of raising stakes, much like Brag or Poker.

Rolling Stone

PLAYERS: FOUR TO SIX

SCORE SHEET: IF NOT GAMBLING

DECK: VARIES ACCORDING TO THE NUMBER OF PLAYERS

ACES: HIGH

ORIGIN: FRANCE

SIMPLICITY FACTOR: 10

SKILL FACTOR: 6

SUITABLE FOR CHILDREN: 7

SUITABLE FOR GAMBLING: 8

This game originated in northern Europe and was called Enfle. It is a quick-paced trick-winning game for between four and six players that is ideal for wagering small amounts.

If being played with four players, all cards below the seven are removed from the deck, if there are five players the sixes and fives are included, if six players then only the twos are removed. Each player is dealt eight cards, there are no trumps and players must follow suit when playing a trick. If any player can't he takes up the other cards that would have made up the trick and incorporates them into his hand. If more than one player can't follow suit the last one in the sequence to play takes up the cards. If everybody follows suit then the trick is gathered up and put aside, to play no further part in proceedings.

The winner is the first player to get rid of all his cards, and he collects one pre-agreed unit from each other player for each card they are left holding. Another unconventional feature of this game is that as soon as a player has played his last card, the game stops, even if it is in the middle of a trick and the cards, quite literally held are the cards to be counted. If not gambling, then the losing players will score a point for each card they are left holding, and after a prearranged time or number of games, the winner will be the one with the least points.

Cribbage

PLAYERS: TWO TO FOUR

DECK: FULL

SCORE SHEET: YES, IF NOT USING A BOARD

ACES: LOW

ORIGIN: GREAT BRITAIN

SIMPLICITY FACTOR: 3

SKILL FACTOR: 8

SU!TABLE FOR CHILDREN: 6

SUITABLE FOR GAMBLING: 7

Dating back to 17th century, Cribbage requires an agile, numerate mind and really ought to be played with a Crib Board (see scoring) to mark the scores as the game progresses. It can be scored with pencil and paper, but the true way to win at cribbage is to be the first to go "twice round the board", scoring 121 points. Essentially a two-handed game, it can be played with three or four but rarely is.

Each player is singly dealt six cards. After inspecting their hand, they each discard two cards that become the "crib". The player who didn't deal cuts the remaining deck and the dealer turns over the top card of the lower half to become the "starter". (This will not be used in the game, but may come into account during the scoring.)

Three of a kind

The non-dealer then plays a card from his hand face-up on the table on his side of the board and calls out its value. The dealer does the same on his side and announces the total value of the two cards. If the first card played was a five, and the second a three, the dealer would call "eight". This goes on until the total amounts to nearly 31, the figure it must not exceed. If the cards in a player's hand will "bust" 31 if played, he calls "Go". The other player must either play a card that will keep it below 31, or make it exactly 31 or call "Go" himself. After that, the cards played are turned face-down, moved to one side and play resumes. If only one player is left holding cards, then he plays them out by himself.

Cards are worth their face value, with court cards counting as ten during the sequence building, and scoring (see below) takes place as this goes on.

After all the cards have been played comes the "show", in which first the non-dealer then the dealer count up the combinations they can make with cards they have played—both can involve the starter in making as many permutations as possible. The dealer then does the same with the crib (again the starter is included) and adds those scores to his own. Following the show, if neither score is at 121 then another six-card hand is dealt, with the non-dealer of the previous round becoming the dealer, and the game continues until one player has been round the board twice.

SCORING

There are two scoring schedules in cribbage, one for points earned during play and one applied to the show.

DURING PLAY

These are points scored for combinations of cards as they are laid on the table. They will involve both players' cards—if one puts down a four of clubs to call "four", then the other plays the four of hearts he will call "eight for a pair" and score two points for the pair. If the first player then plays the four of spades he will call "twelve for three" and score six points for a "royal pair", that is three cards of the same rank which can be made into three different pairs (4H+4S; 4H+4C; 4S+4C).

Ideally, these points would be racked up on the cribbage board (see below). If not a running total must be kept on a score sheet. The schedule of combinations is as follows:

- Pair (two cards of same rank)—2
- Royal Pair (three cards of same rank)—6
- Double Royal Pair (four cards of same rank)—12
- Run (numerical sequence of more than three cards of any suit, not necessarily played in order, so 5H, 3C, 4H, 6D would count)—3 points for making the first three, then one point per card after that
- Flush (cards of any numerical order, but in the same suit)—4 for making the first four, then 1 per card after that
- Running Flush (in numerical order and the same suit)—points are scored for both run and the flush
- Fifteen (the sequence totalling exactly fifteen)—2
- If the starter card is a jack, the dealer scores 2 "for his heels".

THE SHOW

The show is scored in exactly the same way as during play—pairs, runs, flushes and total of fifteen—with first the non-dealer then the dealer making as many combinations as they can from their own hand. All of their cards can be used in as many different combinations as possible, and each player will include the starter as if it were a card they'd been dealt.

If either player's hand includes the jack of the same suit as the starter, they score an extra point. This is called "One for his nob".

THE CRIB

After the dealer has totaled his own show, he will do the same with the four cards that make up the crib, once again involving the start, and adds the score to his own.

A short history of Cribbage

Known for being the only game you can play in an English pub, legally, for money, Cribbage is still widely played today. It is possibly one of the oldest card games, dating back to the 17th century.

The invention of Cribbage is sometimes attributed to the poet Sir John Suckling (1609 - 1642). Suckling was a keen player of cards, dice and bowls as well as being an extravagant gambler and all round party animal. However, there is no hard evidence to prove that Suckling was the inventor of Cribbage, and the rules and other features of the game bear a suspicious resemblance to a number of others and particularly to a game played in Tudor times called Noddy. Sadly, Suckling's wild lifestyle came to an early end. In 1642 he was accused of taking part in a plot to free the Earl of Stafford from the Tower of London. He fled to Paris and is said to have poisoned himself when he was only 32 years old.

The game of cribbage plays a crucial role in Charles Dickens *The Old Curiosity Shop* (1841), and for this reason perhaps is sometimes known as Swiveller's Cribbage, after one of the characters, Richard Swiveller.

PENALTIES

- If a player calls "Go" but could actually have played a card, the cards he is left holding will be removed from play and his opponent scores two points.
- If a player fails to play his cards after his opponent has called "Go", the same penalty applies.
- If a player gets round the board twice before his opponent has got round once, it's called a "lurch" and the winner pegs two games.

A CRIBBAGE BOARD

This is a wooden board with a series of holes divided into two rows of six sets of five. Each player takes a side, moving two pegs up one row and down the other (going

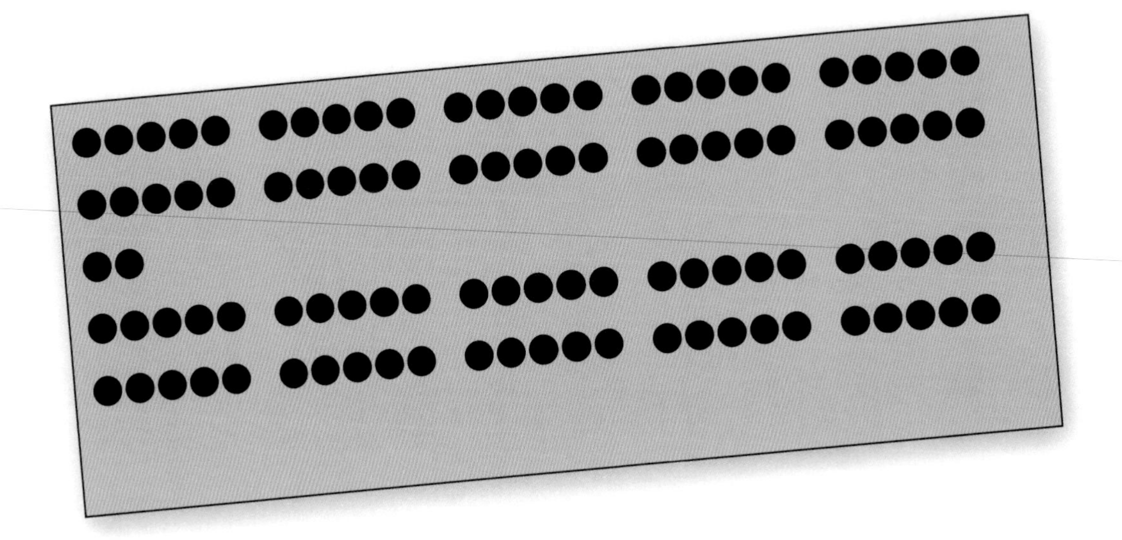

Twice round the board wins the game

round the board). Tally is kept by the pegs being leapfrogged as the totals mount, so if a player scores three points he moves his first peg up three places; then if his next score is two, he'll place the second peg two holes on from that, and so on.
Two extra rows of ten holes in the centre are used to keep track of games won by each player, with a rubber usually lasting until one player has pegged all ten of these holes.

Variations

FIVE- OR SEVEN-HANDED CRIBBAGE

Cribbage can be played with five cards or seven cards. In each case the crib is still made up from two cards from each hand and the rules are exactly the same as for the six-card game. In Five-Handed Cribbage the non-dealer pegs three points for not

having the crib. In Seven-Handed Cribbage games are played to three times round the board or 181 points.

THREE-HANDED CRIBBAGE

Players are dealt five cards and put one each into the crib, which is then dealt one more to bring it up to four. The sequences run round the table with players calling "Go" to the player on their left. Otherwise, the rules are as for the conventional game.

PARTNERSHIP CRIBBAGE

This involves four players in pairs sitting opposite each other. They are dealt five cards each and put one each in the crib. Sequences run round the table, as does the calling of "Go". Points made during play are individual but pegged along the same row on the board and partners' cards are pooled for the show.

Tut!

PLAYERS: 2

DECK: 2 WHOLE (DIFFERENT DESIGNS WITH 2 JOKERS EACH)

SCORE SHEET: YES

SIMPLICITY FACTOR: 6

SKILL FACTOR: 6

SUITABLE FOR CHILDREN: 1

In this game, tactical holding back of certain cards can block your opponent's play, and have them tutting with annoyance.

One player sorts one deck into red and black piles, takes out the jokers, and shuffles each pile. These are placed in the middle of the table.

Meanwhile the other player adds the extra jokers to a second deck and shuffles them. (The jokers will be wild - which means they can represent any card.) This deck is put between the players as the stock. Each player takes one of the half decks (the player who shuffled the stock gets to choose first), and turns over the top card, highest card starts.

The first player takes 5 cards from the stock pile. If there are any aces in this hand, these must be put in the middle as foundations. (The foundations can be built on in numerical order in any suit.) Once all possible cards have been played the player puts one card in front of him, to indicate he has finished. And the other player picks up 5 cards and plays his hand in the same way building on the foundations, and so on.

As the game progresses each player can build up a row of four cards in front of him, that can then be used to progress play, and which are built on in red/black order. If a player can play all 5 cards to the foundations he can pick up 5 more.

As the foundations are completed, i.e. built up to a king, each player takes turns to shuffle the pile and add it to the bottom of the stock pile.

The object is to get rid of the pile of 26 cards. Score by recording how many the loser in each round has left from the pile of 26, first one to 100 is the overall loser.

Vint

PLAYERS: FOUR

DECK: FULL

ACES: HIGH

SCORE SHEET: YES

ORIGIN: RUSSIA

SIMPLICITY FACTOR:
GAME 8–SCORING 5

SKILL FACTOR:
GAME 5–SCORING 5

SUITABLE FOR CHILDREN: 7

SUITABLE FOR GAMBLING: 8

A derivative of Whist which has a few similarities to Bridge, especially in the scoring and bidding processes, Vint originated in Tsarist Russia. The game is played by two teams of two seated opposite each other.

A full deck is dealt out, leaving each player with 13 cards. Once they have inspected their hands, the bidding begins for how many more tricks than "book" (six tricks) they think they can make, nominating their preferred suit as trumps. The highest numerate bid would be "seven", and the suits are, in descending order—no trumps, hearts, diamonds, clubs, spades. "Seven, no trumps" is therefore the highest possible bid.

Unlike in Bridge, there is no dummy in Vint, so both players of the partnership play out the hands as in any Whist-based game. The player who made the successful contract bid leads and once the hand is finished, scoring is very similar to Bridge with a horizontal line drawn across the score sheet and different scores entered "above the line" and "below the line".

SCORING

The partnerships score for the tricks either partner makes. The scores entered below the line are called "game points" and are awarded to each partnership for tricks made during each hand. The amount depends on the value of the contract and are 10 points per trick for a bid of one; 20 points for a bid of two; and so on up to 70 points per trick for a bid of seven. As soon as a partnership reaches 500 below-the-line points the game ends.

Bonus points are entered above the line and are:

- For winning a game—1000
- For winning a rubber (two out of three games)—2000
- For taking 12 tricks in a game (a little slam)—1000
- For taking a little slam if "six" was bid—6000
- For taking 13 tricks in a game (a grand slam)—2000
- For taking a grand slam if "seven" was bid—12000.

Also entered above the line are the following honor points:

Honor cards are the ace, king, queen, jack and ten of trumps and whichever pair has the most of them in the tricks they have won scores ten times the tricks' value for each. If it was a no trumps hand, whichever pair holds the most aces scores 25 times the tricks' value for each—if both partnerships hold two aces in a no trumps round there is no score. The losers' honor cards are not counted.

If any single player holds three aces or a single-suit three-card numerical sequence he scores 500 points for the partnership—either is called a "coronet". If he has the fourth ace he racks up another 500; as does every other card over three in the sequence. If the sequence is in trumps, the scores are doubled to 1000 and it is called a "double coronet".

After one pair has won two games by scoring 500 below the line points twice, the winners of the "rubber" are decided by counting each partnership's total of above- and below-the-line points.

BETTING

A pre-agreed cash value for points system is the best way, with amounts paid on the difference between the winning and losing totals.

Variations

PREFERENCE

A less involved version of Vint, for three players, Preference uses a piquet pack, with no trumps and is much more suitable for gambling. Each player puts a pre-agreed amount in the pot and the deal gives them ten cards each with the remaining two being put aside as the "widow". Bidding then begins for how many tricks each player believes they could make over "book"—in this case five—with their own choice of trumps. The hierarchy of the suits is the same as above. The contract winner effectively plays against the other two, and if he makes the contract he takes money from the pot depending on the value of the contract, for a prearranged amount. If he fails to make it he puts money into the pot at the same value.

Glossary

Aces High: The ace is the highest ranked card in each suit.

Aces Low: The ace is the lowest ranked card in each suit.

Bid: To declare how many tricks a player thinks they will make from that hand.

Carte Blanche: A hand with no picture cards in it.

Cut: Divide the deck in half and place the bottom half on top of the top half. This happens after shuffling but before dealing.

Court Cards: Jack, Queen and King of any suit (see also Face Cards and Picture Cards).

Deal: Distribute the correct number of cards among the players, methods will vary.

Deuce: A two of any suit.

Discards: Cards that players have considered and rejected.

Face Cards: Jack, Queen and King of any suit (see also Court Cards and Picture Cards).

Follow Suit: Play a card of the same suit as the last one played.

Hand: The cards a player holds, or play that results from any one deal.

Knock: To be unable to follow suit and signify thus by knocking the table.

Lead: The first player round the table plays a card and establishes the suit for that hand.

Meld: A group of cards of the same rank or in sequence—usually three cards, but the number varies from game to game.

Misdeal: When the cards are dealt out incorrectly, in which case they will be gathered in, shuffled and redealt.

Pass: To miss your turn when it comes to bidding or playing.

Picture Cards: Jack, Queen and King of any suit (see also Court Card and Face Card).

Piquet Pack: A 32-card deck from which all spot cards lower than the sevens have been removed.

Pot: The amount bet on a hand, collected in the middle of the table or the stack of cards left over from the deal and placed face down on the table to be drawn from.

Rank: A card's numerical or pictorial value, or the order in which these rankings occur.

Revoke: Not following suit.

Slam: A single player or partnership wins all the tricks in one hand.

Spot Cards: Any card, of any suit, ranked from two to ten.

Suit: Hearts, Clubs, Diamonds and Spades are the four suits.

Trey: A three of any suit.

Trick: The cards collected when each player has played a card in accordance of the rules of whatever game is being played.

Trump: A predecided suit that will take preference over all other suits—any trump card will beat any card from any other suit.

Upcard: The card that is turned face-up at the end of a deal to designate trumps.

Wild card: Can be nominated as a card of any value.